Christian
Faith and
Historical
Understanding

About the Author and Respondent

RONALD H. NASH   Ronald Nash is Professor of Philosophy and Head of the Department of Philosophy and Religion at Western Kentucky University (Bowling Green). He is a graduate of Barrington College (B.A.), Brown University (M.A.), and Syracuse University (Ph.D.). He has also taught at Barrington College, Houghton College, and Syracuse University. Dr. Nash is the author or editor of twelve books including: *The Concept of God; Social Justice and the Christian Church; The Word of God and the Mind of Man; Freedom, Justice and the State; Liberation Theology;* and *Ideas of History.*

HAROLD W. HOEHNER   Harold W. Hoehner holds two positions at Dallas Theological Seminary: Director of Th.D. Studies and Department Chairman and Professor of New Testament Literature and Exegesis. After earning his B.A. from Barrington College with honors, he earned a Th.D. at Dallas Theological Seminary, also with honors, and a Ph.D. from King's College at Cambridge University. His published work includes *Chronological Aspects of the Life of Christ, Herod Antipas,* Vol. XVII of the *Society of New Testament Studies Monograph Series,* Vol. XIII of *Studies in Biblical Theology,* several articles for the newly revised *International Standard Bible Encyclopedia,* and other articles in *Bibliotheca Sacra,* the *Zondervan Pictorial Encyclopedia of the Bible,* the *Expositor's Bible Commentary,* and the *Wycliffe Bible Encyclopedia.* He has been listed in the *International Scholars Directory, Who's Who in Religion,* and the *Outstanding Educators of America.*

Christian Faith and Historical Understanding

Ronald H. Nash

with a response by
Harold W. Hoehner

ZONDERVAN PUBLISHING HOUSE
OF THE ZONDERVAN CORPORATION
GRAND RAPIDS, MICHIGAN 49506

PROBE MINISTRIES
INTERNATIONAL
DALLAS, TEXAS 75251

Copyright   © 1984 by Probe Ministries International

Publisher   ACADEMIE BOOKS are printed by Zondervan
Publishing House, 1415 Lake Drive, S.E.,
Grand Rapids, Michigan 49506

Library of   Nash, Ronald H.
Congress   Christian faith and historical understanding.
Cataloging in   Bibliography: p.
Publication Data   1. History (Theology). 2. History—Philosophy.
I. Hoehner, Harold W. II. Title.

BR115.H5N37   1984   901   83-12391
ISBN 0-310-45121-3

Place of   *Printed in the United States of America*
Printing

Design   Book design by Louise Bauer

84 85 86 87 88 89 / 9 8 7 6 5 4 3 2

What Is Probe?

Probe Ministries is a nonprofit corporation organized to provide perspective on the integration of the academic disciplines and historic Christianity. The members and associates of the Probe team are actively engaged in research as well as lecturing and interacting in thousands of university classrooms throughout the United States and Canada on topics and issues vital to the university student.

Christian Free University books should be ordered from Zondervan Publishing House (in the United Kingdom from The Paternoster Press), but further information about Probe's materials and ministries may be obtained by writing to Probe Ministries International, 12011 Coit Road, Suite 107, Dallas, Texas 75251.

Contents

Book Abstract

Christianity claims to be grounded on certain historical events, but some historians question whether any historical events can be known. The author considers the swings that have taken place in nineteenth- and twentieth-century views of history. He shows the effect of these changes on theological thinking, especially in the existential theology of Rudolf Bultmann.

One focus of the book is the question: Is objectivity in history possible? By examining the relation between historical events and interpretations of those events, the author shows the value of a coherence theory of truth in historical thinking, one that seeks a fit with all we know of the past rather than an exact correspondence.

The author approaches the issue of historical knowledge about the resurrection by examining the thoughts of four prominent theologians. The author argues that faith in the resurrection can be grounded on adequate historical evidence. Faith leans on history to provide a solid footing from which the believer can move beyond mere historical knowledge to a faith knowledge that involves personal commitment. The faith of the Christian believer has an inherent historical component. From its inception, Christianity has been a religion with a past. Without that past, Christians can have no grounded hope for the future. At the same time, God calls men and women to move from belief about *to belief* in *the Person who stands both behind history and in it.*

chapter one

History and the Christian Faith

The author distinguishes important senses of the word history *and surveys the rest of the book.*

Because Christianity has a unique relationship to history, the topics discussed in this book should be matters of concern to both believers and nonbelievers. For one thing, Christianity teaches that God has revealed Himself in history. As American theologian William Hordern observes, "Whereas other religions have looked to nature and mystical or rational experience to find the revelation of God, the Biblical faith finds revelation primarily in certain historical events."[1] Historian Herbert Butterfield explains that Christianity is a historical religion because "it presents us with religious doctrines which are at the same time historical events or historical interpretations."[2] Butterfield goes on to note: "Certain historical events are held to be part of the [Christian] religion itself— they are considered to have a spiritual content and to

11

represent the divine breaking in upon history."[3] Christians believe that in Jesus Christ God actually entered into human history.

Christianity is also a historical religion in the sense that the actual occurrence of certain events like the crucifixion and the resurrection is a necessary condition for its truth. If such an event as the resurrection of Christ can be shown to have happened in history, many Christians believe, important Christian claims will be vindicated. Some Christian thinkers go so far as to claim that historical evidence can actually prove the truth of many Christian beliefs. While others insist that the evidence falls short of definitive proof, they agree that history can provide evidence that makes the faith of individual Christian believers reasonable. But the appeal to historical evidence is a coin with two sides. Nonbelievers get equally excited about the possibility that historical evidence might falsify essential Christian claims. British theologian T. A. Roberts is correct when he states, "The truth of Christianity is anchored in history: hence the implicit recognition that if some or all of the events upon which Christianity has been traditionally thought to be based could be proved unhistorical, then the religious claims of Christianity would be seriously jeopardized."[4] Another British writer, Alan Richardson, agrees:

> The Christian faith is thus an historical faith, in the sense that it is more than the mere intellectual acceptance of a certain kind of theistic philosophy; it is bound up with certain happenings in the past, and if these happenings could be shown never to have occurred, or to have been quite different from the biblical-Christian account of them, then the whole edifice of Christian faith, life and worship would be found to have been built on sand.[5]

Clearly, then, questions about the relationship between Christianity and history should not be taken lightly.

What Is History?

The word *history* is ambiguous. It may be used to refer to events that happened in the past or it may mean the narrative, account, or record of the past. That is, history can refer either to that which is studied (the past) or to the study itself. In this book we will be concerned primarily with the second sense of history—that is, the historian's record of the past, the narrative that connects past events and makes them intelligible.

Several more distinctions are necessary, however, if the essence of history is to be made clear. For one thing, we must distinguish between the past as such and the *human* past. While there may be other disciplines (like paleontology) that may be interested in the prehuman past, history is concerned with the past of humankind. Second, an important difference exists between just any event in the human past and *significant* events. Consider the hypothetical fact that at 9:04 A.M. on December 29, 1520, King Henry VIII of England sneezed. Events such as this are not the proper concern of history. The historian is concerned with past events that are significant, such as, for example, the fact that in 1531 A.D. Henry VIII declared himself head of the English church. In most cases, a sneeze (even the sneeze of a king) is not important enough to warrant inclusion in a historical record. Had Henry's sneeze been severe enough to rupture a blood vessel and thus cause paralysis or death, it would have been significant. History, then, is concerned only with the important things that have happened in the human past. The trivial, the commonplace, and the insignificant are not grist for the mill of history.

Still another distinction that must be noted is the difference between two possible kinds of records about the significant human past, a distinction that played a prominent role in the thought of the Italian philosopher Benedetto Croce. A historian's record of the past may be either a *chronicle* (a simple narrative) or a *significant narrative*. A chronicle is a mere record of events in their chronological order without any statement about their significance or connection. A chronicle gives what British philosopher W. H. Walsh calls a "simple narrative," whereas history is concerned to provide "a significant narrative." In Walsh's words, "The historian is not content to tell us merely what happened; he wishes to make us see why it happened, too. In other words, he aims . . . at a reconstruction of the past which is both intelligent and intelligible."[6]

Taking all the distinctions we have made into account, we may define history as *the attempt to reconstruct in a significant narrative the important events of the human past through a study of the relevant data available in the historian's own present experience.* The definition stipulates that the data on which the historian constructs his narrative are found in the historian's own present experience. This point, easily misunderstood, simply means that historical evidence in the form of earlier documents and artifacts cannot become a source for the historian until he knows it. The events studied by the historian no longer exist. The only way a historian who is working in his present knows that *x* occurred in the past is by information about *x* being preserved in some historical record. This means that the historian's access to the past must always proceed through the instrumentality of some record of the past. This evidence or record that exists in the historian's present is his way of gaining access to a past that no longer exists.

For several decades now, many Christian theologians have used two different German words for history *(Historie* and *Geschichte)*—to make still another distinction.* American theologian Carl E. Braaten explains

> *Historie* is the sum total of historical facts lying "back there" in the past which can be objectively verified; the mode of knowledge appropriate here is impartial investigation and neutral observation. *Geschichte* has to do with phenomena that concern me existentially, that make some demand upon me and call for commitment; the mode of knowledge with exclusive right at this level is existential experience-acknowledgement.[7]

---

*The technical theological usage of *Historie* and *Geschichte* we are noting apparently originated with Martin Kähler's book, *Der soggenannte historische Jesus und der geschichtliche biblische Christus,* published in 1892. An important caveat: the reader should not assume that the properties of *Historie* as described by Carl Braaten (objective facts lying in a dead past discoverable through impartial investigation) are universally accepted. A later chapter of this book will question the adequacy of the view Braaten describes.

According to theologian James Peter, *"Historie*
means the study of past events with a view to discovering in an objective detached manner what actually happened. *Geschichte* on the other hand means
the study of past events in such a way that the discovery of what happened calls for decision on our
part."[8] John Macquarrie, Professor of Divinity at
Oxford University, translates *Historie* and *Geschichte* respectively as "objective-historical" and
"existential-historical."[9] One way to visualize the
distinction is to imagine two veterans of America's
War Between the States, a Yankee and a Confederate,
who return to the battlefield at Gettysburg years after
the decisive battle. Standing together, say, at Ceme-
tery Ridge, they can agree on the *Historie* of what had
taken place there years before. But for each of them,
the *Geschichte,* the existential significance of what
happened, would be quite different. Likewise, a believer and an unbeliever may agree on the *Historie* of
Christ's crucifixion. But the existential significance of
that event (its *Geschichte*) for an orthodox Christian
who believes that Christ's death was God's atonement
for his sin and the only possible ground of his
justification will obviously be different from what it is
for the person who may regard Jesus only as a human
being who was executed for treason or blasphemy.
According to Braaten:

> In historical research there is apparently a theologically
> neutral level of discovering, examining, and criticizing,
> by various objective criteria, documents of history and
> ascertaining from them a body of so-called factual mate-
> rial. But at some point the question of meaning, of in-
> terpretation, arises which no historian can escape. His
> interpretation will be guided by presuppositions which
> are so much a part of him that he cannot suspend them at
> will. Existentialist historiography has highlighted this
> dimension of meaning, the inescapability of presupposi-
> tions in interpretation, the historian's involvement with
> history, the demand for decision and responsible action
> in relation to the historical texts to which they are in some
> way purportedly joined. It is as if the facts in themselves
> are neutral, meaningless, and dumb, as if interpretations
> have to be imported from the outside, arbitrarily imposed
> upon the facts from the value-creating subjectivity of the

historian. Sooner or later the thought will occur that since meanings do not arise *from* the facts, they do not need to rest *on* the facts; meanings can stand on their own feet, and facts can be handed on to those who are entertained by archaeological studies.[10]

Braaten's comments raise a number of important questions.* For one, Is *Historie* as objective and impartial as he seems to suggest? Suppose it is not. Would this blur the distinction between *Historie* and *Geschichte?* What does he mean when he suggests that the meanings of historical facts do not arise *from* the facts? Students of liberal Christian theology know how various liberal theologians attempted to deny the historicity of certain events (their status as *Historie*) while attempting to preserve value for them as *Geschichte*. Pastors and theologians who were completely convinced that the resurrection of Christ was not a real event in history still loved to preach Easter sermons about "the resurrection." In those sermons they were engaged in the strange enterprise of seeking existential significance *(Geschichte)* in an event that had never happened *(Historie)*. This is not to say that the distinction between *Historie* and *Geschichte* should be abandoned. But much more careful attention needs to be given to the nature of each, to their relationship with each other (can something be *Geschichte* without there being a corresponding event in *Historie?*), and to their respective relationships to personal belief or trust.

**The Plan
of This Book**

The inherent connection between history and the Christian faith gives rise to a number of problems that are treated in this book. Chapter 2 examines the highly influential nineteenth-century attempt to make history scientific. The search for the facts and laws of history led to a distorted view of the historian's ex-

---

*Once again a warning is necessary. I quote Braaten's paragraph to illustrate the way in which some contemporary thinkers use the distinction between *Historie* and *Geschichte*. Many of the claims made in Braaten's quote will be evaluated critically later in this study. Readers interested in Karl Barth's use of *Historie* and *Geschichte* may consult his *Church Dogmatics* III.1.84 and III.2.535.

pertise that was soon discarded. Chapter 2 will also consider the impact the scientific model of history had on studies of the life of Jesus.

Chapter 3 surveys the idealistic reaction of thinkers like Wilhelm Dilthey and R. G. Collingwood to the scientific approach to history. Their emphasis on the role that the subjectivity of the historian plays in historical understanding had its corollary in Christian theology. The idealist's turn away from the outer world of historical fact to the inner world of the historian's subjectivity influenced Christian existentialists who disparaged history in favor of subjective decision and self-knowledge.

Chapter 4 focuses on the theology of the famous German theologian Rudolf Bultmann. Bultmann's position with regard to Christianity and history has been so influential that even those who reject his views are often forced to begin their treatment of many topics with a consideration of his writings.

Chapter 5 asks the question, "Can history be objective?" The problem is at the same time one of the most important and vexing questions in the philosophy and theology of history. In this chapter I discuss the ways in which the various answers to the question affect Christian apologetics and theology. I also offer my own answer to the question.

Chapter 6 deals with a related set of issues: Are there facts of history and, if so, what are they? Many students of history manifest what may be called the Sergeant Friday Syndrome. Like the famous policeman of the *Dragnet* television show of the 1950s, they regard historical investigation as a simple matter of *getting the facts*. As it turns out, however, getting the facts is not as easy as some people think. For one thing, considerable disagreement continues over even the exact nature of a historical fact.

In chapter 7 many of the points raised in earlier chapters are brought to bear on the crucial matter of the resurrection of Christ. Six basic questions about the resurrection and its relation to history are asked. The answers of four different twentieth-century theologians—Bultmann, Karl Barth, Wolfhart Pannenberg, and George Ladd—are then noted and evaluated.

Chapter 8 takes a detailed look at the interrelationship between the personal faith of individual believers and history. Is personal Christian faith dependent on history? As I point out, the question is a complex one and its answer requires a careful investigation of a number of related issues.

chapter two

Scientific History and the Historical Jesus

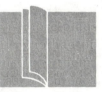

In this chapter the author describes historical positivism and its attempts to produce a true and objective account of the past. He also examines the influence of positivist assumptions on those theologians and historians who engaged in the "search for the historical Jesus."

When scientists, historians, and philosophers first began to study the methodological problems of the natural and social sciences in the nineteenth century, they divided generally into two camps—positivism and idealism. The attitude of nonevangelical theology* to the importance and reliability of the New Testament as a historical record has, over the past one hundred and fifty years, reflected one or the other of

---

*In this book, "evangelical" refers to a Protestant Christian who accepts the traditional (orthodox) beliefs of the Christian faith, who believes human beings need to be brought into a personal saving relationship with God through Jesus Christ, and who accepts the Bible as the ultimate authority on Christian belief and practice. 19

those competing approaches. It is difficult if not impossible to understand the twentieth-century debate over Christianity's relationship to history without knowing something about the differences between positivism and idealism. Also important is the way that convictions from those philosophies of history influenced the perception of history among Christian theologians. This chapter will concentrate on *historical positivism* and the most important manifestation of a scientific model of history within Christian thought: the "search for the historical Jesus." In chapter 3 we will focus on historical idealism and its influence on the thought of Christian existentialists like Rudolf Bultmann.

The historical positivists argued that there are *no essential differences between any of the legitimate branches of human knowledge.* In their approach to history, the positivists conceded that history can never provide man with certain knowledge. But, they maintained, this was not due to the nature of history itself but to the methods used by historians in trying to understand the past. *The nineteenth-century positivists sought new methods that would put history on a firm scientific basis.* First of all, they insisted that history should be approached in such a way as to avoid the uncritical and inexact work of earlier historians. The German historian Leopold von Ranke (1795–1886) urged historians to describe the past "as it actually happened" *(wie es eigentlich gewesen).*[11] At the University of Berlin Ranke helped train many of the leading historians of the nineteenth century. He stressed that all sources be critically evaluated, with the emphasis placed on using primary sources as the key evidence. Ranke affirmed the possibility of a true and objective account of the past. For him, the purpose of history was simple: gather the evidence, evaluate it, and then tell the truth about the human past. The historian should set aside his opinions and prejudices and describe the past as it really happened. The primary virtues of Ranke's historian were *detachment, impartiality,* and *objectivity.* Just forget your prejudices, get the facts, and report the truth: this is what historical writing was all about for Ranke and his followers.

Second, like British historian Henry Thomas Buckle (1821–1862). the positivist claimed that history could be made scientific by assuming that *there are universal laws that govern social activity and that the regularity of human conduct can be discovered by statistical means*. The dramatic advances made by the natural sciences after Galileo were a result of the discovery of the laws governing the natural universe. The social sciences could never attain the respect of the natural sciences until the laws that operated in their disciplines were discovered. For this reason, positivist historians in the nineteenth century embarked on a search for what they believed would be the "iron laws" that control human history. Their goal was to turn history into a legitimate science. The fact that there are general laws governing history and that these laws can be discovered inductively was one important thesis of Buckle's *History of Civilization in England* (1857). He wrote, "The great truth that the actions of men, being guided by their antecedents, are in reality never inconsistent, but, however capricious they may appear, only form part of one vast scheme of universal order . . . is at once the key and the basis of history."

Buckle had been influenced by the earlier work of the French philosopher and sociologist Auguste Comte (1798–1857), the founder of positivism and, by all accounts, its most important representative. Comte argued that his positivistic philosophy was superior to any competitive system because it recognized that all phenomena are subject to uniform natural laws. He believed that truth could be discovered only through the use of the scientific method. Comte's *Course de philosophie positive* (published in six volumes between 1830 and 1842) became a manifesto for later positivists. Comte argued that human knowledge has passed in order through three stages: the theological, the metaphysical, and the scientific (or positivistic).

In the theological stage, man explained natural phenomena in terms of divine activity; in the metaphysical stage, he attributed changes in nature to abstract forces; but when he finally attains the stage of science (or positivism), he explains phenomena in terms of the unchanging laws of nature. Comte believed that every area of human knowledge either has passed or will pass through these stages. While some of these areas (such as the study of nature) have attained the positive stage, others, such as the study of history and social phenomena, have lagged behind. Comte felt that he could do for the social sciences what Galileo, Kepler, and Newton had done for the natural sciences. What Comte desired for every branch of human learning was the discovery of the one fundamental law that ties its phenomena together in the same way that Newton's discovery of gravitation unified the study of physics. After Comte, the quest for uniform natural laws governing events in history became a dominant characteristic of the positivist approach to history. While some contemporaries of the nineteenth-century positivists may have applauded their goals and sincere effort, few believed that any of the positivists had succeeded in identifying the iron laws of history.

Viewed from the perspective of the late twentieth century, the positivist search for the iron laws of history is a curio of nineteenth-century thought, while Ranke's call for the historian to eliminate his own subjectivity in a passionless search for the facts is dismissed as a noble dream. The nineteenth-century model of a scientific history was too simplistic to carry the day once its inadequacies were laid bare by historical idealists like Wilhelm Dilthey and R. G. Collingwood. But while it lasted, the ideal of a scientific history exercised a considerable and unfortunate influence on liberal Christian theology. *In an important sense, the nineteenth-century quest for the historical Jesus presumed the relevance and possibility of a scientific history of the life and teachings of Jesus.* Ranke's concern to discover the past as it really was became an obsession of biblical scholars. This obsession, coupled with the skeptical conviction that the Gospels were not historically reliable, caused scholars to do everything possible to reconstruct what they believed to be an unbiased and objective picture of the historical Jesus.

"The historical Jesus" is a technical phrase. The so-called problem of the historical Jesus concerns what can be known about Jesus, using only the methods of "scientific" (positivist) history. The historical Jesus, then, is not identical with the Jesus described in the Bible; it is the Jesus who can be known by means of the historico-critical method as applied to the sources of life and teaching of Jesus. Before anyone became aware that there might be any problem about the historical Jesus, most Protestants and Catholics took the biblical picture of Jesus as historically accurate. While they were aware of the difficulties of reconciling some parallel accounts in the different Gospels, the problems were thought to be minor. There was little doubt that the Gospels should be read as a historical account of Jesus; there was general acceptance that this account was a faithful historical record of what had happened.

Several factors helped give rise to nineteenth-century attempts to discover the "real" Jesus:

1. One of the most important of these factors was a growing spirit of distrust about the traditional Christian picture of Jesus, a skepticism in keeping with the drift of Western thought following the Enlightenment. Many assumed that the Gospels could no longer be read as reliable historical documents whose picture of Jesus could be accepted at face value. For such thinkers, the Gospel records contained errors, myths, and even outright lies that needed to be stripped away by the methods of literary and historical criticism. Carl Braaten suggests "that the nineteenth century historians wanted a kind of photographic replica of Jesus which could be had, it was assumed, by wiping away the filmy coatings that later tradition had placed upon him."[12] But most of these scholars did not expect the photographic replica to resemble very closely the Jesus portrayed in the Gospels.

2. Another factor in the quest for the historical Jesus involved those scholars taking part. They were for the most part children of the Enlightenment. They regarded autonomous human reason as the ultimate test of truth. Further, they were controlled by a rationalism and naturalism that doubted the miracu-

The Problem of "the Historical Jesus"

lous and spurned the supernatural. They believed that a discovery of the historical Jesus would enable them to dispense once and for all with the supernatural Jesus of traditional Christianity.

3. Consequently, liberal biographers of Jesus assumed that the reference to any miraculous or supernatural event in the Gospels was sufficient evidence to establish the unhistorical nature of the material. As British theologian I. Howard Marshall points out, "Many of these investigators believed that the real Jesus must have been an ordinary person with nothing supernatural or divine about him. His life must have conformed to ordinary human patterns, and be explicable in purely human categories. For such people the phrase "the historical Jesus' clearly meant a non-supernatural Jesus."[13] In other words, this third factor in the quest has to do with the all-pervading naturalistic presuppositions of the historians and theologians who were involved. Their a priori position was one that *assumed* Jesus could not have had supernatural capabilities.

4. The fourth factor in the nineteenth-century quest is this: It proceeded in the spirit of Ranke's search for the past "as it really was." The advocates of this quest thought it was both possible and desirable to discover the simple facts about Jesus, stripped of any interpretations that the early church had added to its picture of Jesus.

Hence the nineteenth-century participants in the quest for the historical Jesus thought the real person who lay at the end of the search would turn out to be a Jesus compatible with their liberal theology. Theological liberals in the nineteenth century had an obvious problem with traditional Protestant and Catholic teaching about Jesus. They did not believe Christ was divine; they rejected the traditional doctrine of his incarnation; many of them rejected the traditional doctrines of the atonement and bodily resurrection. Many of the liberals were humanists who wanted a totally human Jesus who was important primarily because of his *ethical* teaching. They wanted to throw off the theological and metaphysical interpretations of Jesus found in the writings of Paul and in the early Christian creeds. These scholars were convinced that the picture of the historical Jesus that would emerge from their historical research would provide a ground on which the Christian religion could be purified of its embarassing supernaturalism and metaphysical dogmas. They envisioned a ground that would make possible a renewal of Christianity in the eyes of "modern" man. With these assumptions in view, the various liberal biographies of Jesus picked their way through the source materials so as to leave a picture of Jesus compatible with liberalism's humanism and naturalism. The historical Jesus, it was thought, would turn out to be not the Jesus of Protestant conservatives or Roman Catholic traditionalists, but the Jesus of liberal theology.

It did not take long for critics of the liberal quest for the historical Jesus to see through the pretentiousness of liberal historical scholarship. While liberals denigrated the historical value of the Gospels as the biased work of committed partisans, it soon became obvious that their own reconstruction of Jesus was anything but objective. It became clear that liberal participants in the quest "discovered" precisely what they *wanted* to discover. As one early critic put it, the Christ that the liberal sees "looking back through nineteen centuries of Catholic darkness, is only the reflection of a liberal Protestant face, seen at the bottom of a deep well."[14] Decades later, Carl Braaten would make the same point:

> The nineteenth-century biographers of Jesus were like plastic surgeons making over the face of their patient in their own image, or like an artist who paints himself in the figures he creates. There was, in most cases, unmistakable resemblance between their portrayal of the religion of Jesus and their own personal religious stance. It also happened that the scholar usually found about as much as he was looking for. That is to say, he found out as much about Jesus, allegedly on purely historical grounds, as he needed to prop up his own theology.[15]

And so the liberal quest for the historical Jesus was discredited as being, not an objective and unbiased search for the basic facts about Jesus, but an enterprise prejudiced from the very start, in which those involved in the search found exactly what they were looking for.

A number of other forces bearing on the quest revealed once and for all the hopelessness of the liberal search.* For our purposes, the most important of these was the rise of a competing and more realistic appraisal of historical understanding. British theologian T. A. Roberts explains:

> The nineteenth-century quests for the historical Jesus worked on what now can be seen to be a mistaken and erroneous conception of historical method. It presupposed the possibility of recovering historical "facts" devc⁣d of interpretation, and in the context of the historical examination of the gospels this meant the recovery of plain historical facts about Jesus divorced from the theological interpretations, the dogmas and doctrines, in which those facts are embedded in the gospels as they now stand.[16]

Historians became convinced that Ranke's model of scientific history was much too simple to do justice to the historian's enterprise.

> The truth is that in an age of revolutionary change, and therefore of historical reappraisal, twentieth-century historians found themselves abandoning the nineteenth-century notion of "scientific history" not for philosophical reasons but for historical ones. When it was discovered that neither Ranke himself nor anyone else had written presuppositionless history, and that behind the laboratory-jackets of the "scientific historians" were disguised the "wise men of the tribe" spinning their myths, it was sensibly concluded, not that Ranke and his fellow workers were not historians, but that the theory which represented history as an objectively factual science, like the physical sciences, must be wrong. Twentieth-century historians have, in truth, learnt from the course of events themselves what the nineteenth-century histories, by and large, failed to learn from [Ed-

---

*These include the important critique contained in Albert Schweitzer's book *The Quest of the Historical Jesus: A Critical Study of Its Progress from Reimarus to Wrede* (London: A & C Black, 1910) and the rise of form-criticism. That story has been told many times by others. See for example the account in I. Howard Marshall, *I Believe in the Historical Jesus* (Grand Rapids: Eerdmans, 1977), chapter 6.

mund] Burke. Contemporary historians for the most part have abandoned positivist conceptions of history for the same reasons that in an earlier revolutionary age Burke and his followers had abandoned the rationalist conception of history of Hume and the *Philosophes*.[17]

As historians lost confidence in the possibility of attaining total objectivity and of separating fact from interpretation, they naturally lost interest in the search for the simple facts about Jesus freed of all theological interpretation. A consensus opinion began to develop "that the attempt of Protestant liberalism to discover the Jesus of history, in contrast to the Christ of faith, was naïve and illegitimate. . . ."[18] *The very conception of history that served as the foundation of the liberal quest came to be viewed as obsolete.*

Traditional Christians could welcome the news that the scientific model of history and the liberal quest grounded on that model were dead. But this did not mean that they necessarily could take comfort in every feature of the new model of history and its use by Christian theologians. While one battle may have ended, the war continued on a different field of combat. The liberalism that collapsed in the early decades of the twentieth century was followed by the neoorthodoxy of Karl Barth and the existentialism of thinkers like Rudolf Bultmann. Nonevangelical theology in the twentieth century found historical idealism more to its liking. But this posed a new set of challenges to those concerned with the tie of Christian truth to history.

chapter three

Historical Idealism and the Existentialist Jesus

The development of historical idealism in the works of Dilthey and Collingwood is examined. Their response to positivism made evident the historian's need to understand the events of history. Walsh's and Dray's correctives are then presented to demonstrate the historian's need to provide a framework for understanding the seemingly irrational events of history.

The oversimplification of Ranke's search for the brute facts of the past and the excesses of the positivist quest for the iron laws of history made the reaction of historical idealists like Wilhelm Dilthey, Benedetto Croce, and R. G. Collingwood inevitable. Their backlash had its theological corollary in the existentialism of thinkers like Rudolf Bultmann. As Carl Braaten notes, "Existentialism is the reverse side of positivism." The existentialist fails to find any meaning in history and thus "flees into the inwardness of the self as the alternate locus of meaning."[19] Braaten says further,

29

The existentialist view of history arose as a response to nineteenth-century positivistic historiography which searched the past for "brute facts," ordered them in causal sequence, and called that history. This history could be reconstructed only by a historical scientist who remained objective, impartial, and disinterested over against his material. As a truly scientific man, the historian must have no ax to grind, no propaganda to make, and no philosophical presuppositions guiding his inquiry. The existentialists realized that there was more to history than that.[20]

Historical idealists disagreed with the positivists over the nature of historical understanding. While the positivists argued that explanation must have the same logical structure in all areas of human knowledge, the idealists countered that explanation in history is quite different from explanation in the natural sciences. Wilhelm Dilthey* set out to produce a "Critique of Historical Reason" that would do for history what Immanuel Kant's critiques of pure and practical reason had done for mathematics, science, and ethics. While Dilthey's work was never completed, he did leave behind a considerable body of writing that criticized positivism and pointed historians in a new direction. He attempted to find a new foundation for historical understanding that would rescue history from the misguided efforts of the positivists while still preserving its status as an empirical and objective branch of knowledge.

One of Dilthey's major concerns was to define and defend the autonomy of history as an independent branch of human knowledge. He maintained that there were two distinct kinds of science: the natural sciences *(Naturwissenschaften)* and the human sciences *(Geisteswissenschaften)*. While the positivists had sought to reduce every branch of human knowledge to the model of the natural sciences, Dilthey insisted that the human or social sciences were distinct and irreducible branches of knowledge. For him, a division of human knowledge can be legitimate even

*Wilhelm Dilthey (1833–1911) was a professor of philosophy at the universities of Basel (1866–68), Kiel (1868–71), Breslau (1871–82), and Berlin (from 1882 until his retirement).

if it is not subsumable under the methods of the natural sciences. As Dilthey saw it, positivism seemed "to mutilate historical reality in order to adapt it to the ideas and methods of the natural sciences."*

One major difference between the natural and human sciences is the way they approach their subject matter. The natural sciences come at their subject matter from the outside, as it were. The natural sciences describe regularities in nature through an observation of natural phenomena. When a scientist observes a ball rolling down an incline or planets sweeping through the heavens, what he studies is obviously quite distinct from himself. He cannot become part of what he studies; he cannot enter into it. He can only look at the outside of what he is studying. In the human sciences, however, the subject matter is accessible to the social scientist in a way not possible in the natural sciences. Because the historian is a human being studying the actions of other human beings, he can know their actions from the inside. Thus a much closer identification between scientist and subject is possible in the social sciences. Since a complete knowledge of the past requires a knowledge both of what happened and why it happened, the historian is often required to "relive" or "rethink" the actions of the past through a process Dilthey called *Verstehen*. Therefore, the social sciences, unlike the natural sciences, have an inner or conscious dimension that can be known immediately through the process of *Verstehen*.

There is yet another difference between the natural and human sciences in Dilthey's philosophy. While the natural scientist searches for regularities in nature

---

*Dilthey's *Einleitung in de Geistenwissenschaften (Introduction to the Human Sciences)* was published in 1883. Dilthey never completed the systematic work he longed to write, but his major essays on the subject were edited and published posthumously under the title *Critik her historischen Vernunft*. Many of his important comments on history appear in translation in H. P. Rickman's collection, *Pattern and Meaning in History* (New York: Harper & Row, 1962). A brief but representative sample of his views can be found in Volume 2 of Ronald Nash's *Ideas of History* (New York: Dutton, 1969). The quote corresponding to this note appears in Nash, *Ideas,* p. 26.

and for generalizations that he can make about these regularities, the historian studies something that is unique, individual, and nonrepeatable. The events of history occur but once. Obviously, lawlike generalizations about unique and nonrepeatable events appear out of reach. This unique feature of historical events created something of a dilemma for Dilthey. In order to explain the past, he recognized, it is necessary that the human sciences rise above subjectivity and individuality and attain some degree of objectivity and universality. The nineteenth-century positivists grounded the universal character of historical knowledge in universal laws. But as we have seen, this amounted to a reductionism in which the social sciences were subordinated to natural sciences such as physics.

Since Dilthey rejected the reductionism of the positivists, he had to find some other way of freeing history from any taint of subjectivity. He did this by postulating what he called Objective Mind. In his view, the human spirit becomes objectified in certain visible phenomena such as language, literature, laws, architecture, religion, music, tools, art, towns, and so on. In Dilthey's words, Objective Mind means

> the manifold forms in which the common background subsisting among various individuals has objectified itself in the sensible world. In this objective mind the past is for us a permanent enduring present. Its realm extends from the style of life and the forms of economic intercourse to the whole system of ends which society has formed for itself, to morality, law, the State, religion, art, science and philosophy.[21]

This Objective Mind includes everything that exhibits some aspect of the spirit of a civilization or culture. The historian can study these objective expressions of man's mind in the past and through them he can enter into and "relive" the human experiences of the past. This experience of reliving the past is *not optional* for the historian. *Unless one enters imaginatively and sympathetically into the thought processes and inner life of the people who lived in the past, it will be impossible to understand that past.* This intellectual reliving of the past is possible because the inner life of past human beings appears in an objectified form in the Objective Mind. Obviously, then, Dilthey believed that one major fault of much prior reflection about the foundations of history was a failure to relate history properly to the data of human consciousness. Too often, he argued, the study of historical phenomena was isolated from the inner world of consciousness. For Dilthey, the only secure and certain historical knowledge is that found in inner experience, in the facts of consciousness.

While Dilthey responded to positivism in Germany, Benedetto Croce of Italy represented another important idealist reaction to the scientific (positivist) model of history.* Croce regarded the Rankean ideal of history as pseudohistory, as a history "without truth or passion." Ranke's insistence that the historian lay aside all personal interest in the pursuit of total impartiality was not only absurd for Croce, it also entailed a serious distortion of history. Ranke's ideal of an objective account of the past ignores the unavoidable present interests of the historian. Moreover, a bare recitation of past events is not even history; it is something else that Croce called chronicle.

Croce's distinction between history and chronicle has become a permanent fixture in contemporary discussions about history.[22] A chronicle is dead history, a corpse of history. A chronicle is *dead* in the sense that it does not live in the thought or experience of the historian. True history is *alive* because the historian, in understanding the past, relives it in his own mind. Historical sources may be alive or dead as well. Anyone who has visited the British Museum and watched an untutoted person stare at a source like the Rosetta Stone† without comprehending its historical sig-

---

*Croce (1860–1952) was not a professor. Although he served twice as Minister of Education in Italy, he was able to spend most of his life in literary work.

†The Rosetta stone is a stone tablet on which an Egyptian decree of 196 B.C. was inscribed in three languages: Greek, Egyptian hieroglyphic, and Demotic. Discovered near the Egyptian town of Rosetta in 1799, this important archaeological find provided the key to deciphering Egyptian hieroglyphics.

nificance has witnessed something of what Croce had in mind. Documents and artifacts must become alive in the present experience of the historian before they can become historical sources. In the process of reliving the past, the historian gives life to his sources. A dead chronicle may become history as it becomes alive: a history may become a dead chronicle as it dies.

Dilthey's Objective Mind and Croce's distinction between history and chronicle were important developments in the idealists' response to the positivist model of history. Even more important has been the work of the English scholar R. G. Collingwood.* Collingwood's opposition to historical positivism was grounded primarily on his conviction that the historian does not explain natural phenomena as the natural scientist does, but attempts to explain the actions of free human beings who order their actions in accordance with reason. Therefore, according to Collingwood, in investigating past events, the historian must make a distinction between the inside and the outside of an event.

> By the outside of the event I mean everything belonging to it which can be described in terms of bodies and their movements: the passage of Caesar, accompanied by certain men, across a river called the Rubicon at one date, or the spilling of his blood on the floor of the senate house at another. By the inside of the event I mean that in it which can only be described in terms of thought: Caesar's defiance of Republican law, or the clash of constitutional policy between himself and his assassins.[23]

Collingwood's distinction between the inner and outer dimensions of the past was paralleled by a difference between *actions* and *events:* an event is anything that happened in the past. An action is an event that had an inner side. The historian, according to Collingwood, should not ignore either facet of the past, the inside or the outside. But it is crucial to see that the historian does more than study mere events; he studies actions that are a *unity* of the outside and

---

*Collingwood (1889–1943) was a professor at Oxford University in England.

the inside of events. While nature is always a mere phenomenon to the scientist, the events of history are more; they are never just spectacles presented for the historian to observe. The historian does not look *at* the events of history; rather he looks *through* them to discern the thought behind them. To illustrate his point, Collingwood compared the work of an archaeologist with that of a paleontologist. While both spend much of their time digging, they dig for different reasons. The paleontologist isn't interested in any thought behind his relics, for there is none. He is interested in the past but is not doing history. The archaeologist, on the other hand, uses his relics as a way of reconstructing the inner thought-life of the people who used the artifacts; he views his relics as clues to how people in the past lived and thought. For Collingwood, history can be known because it is a manifestation of human thought. But in order to understand the past, the historian must know what the agents of history thought when they performed their deeds; and in order to know what they thought, the historian must rethink their thoughts in his own mind.

To summarize, Collingwood thought that historical investigation has two dimensions. If the historian focuses only on the outer side, what takes place in the physical world (the bare event), he is not doing his job properly. The historian's *primary task* is to think his way into the action, into the inner side of the event. To do this, he must recreate the event in his own mind. In Collingwood's words,

> Historical knowledge is the knowledge of what mind has done in the past, and at the same time it is the redoing of this, the perpetuation of past acts in the present. Its object is therefore not a mere object, something outside the mind which it knows; it is an activity of thought, which can be known only in so far as the knowing mind re-enacts it and knows itself as so doing. To the historian, the activities whose history he is studying are not spectacles to be watched, but experiences to be lived through in his own mind; they are objective, or known to him, only because they are also subjective, or activities of his own.[24]

If Collingwood's approach to history is accepted, it follows that "all history is the history of thought."[25]

Moreover, the only way in which the historian can discover the thoughts that constitute the essence of history is "by rethinking them in his own mind."[26] The historian must strive to reenact the past thoughts of historical agents in his own mind. The historian then is not simply a passive observer embarked on a discovery of the past. He is an active agent who, because of his necessary involvement with his subject matter, is in a sense reconstructing the past.

Contemporary Revisions of Collingwood's Work

Even Collingwood's most sympathetic interpreters recognize the need for major revisions of his position. Attention has been directed to two problems in particular. One of these problems centers on whether the notion of thought in Collingwood's claim that the historian must rethink the past should be understood in a narrow or in a broad sense. Collingwood seems to have taken the word *thought* in its most narrow sense as referring only to such rational dimensions of human life as thinking and reasoning. But this creates a major difficulty for his position since it suggests that the only human actions that can be understood by the historian are those that were deliberate. It seems obvious that many highly significant historical acts were done spontaneously without prior reflection or thought. In such cases, the historian striving to rethink the past has absolutely nothing to rethink. But this would make such an event as the martyrdom of Thomas Becket (1118–1170) unintelligible. Understood in Collingwood's narrow sense of "thought," the drunken outburst of England's Henry II that led to Becket's murder was not a rational act in the sense of being calculated or intentional. It was an irrational outburst of anger and resentment by a drunken man. If all history is indeed the history of thought and if the word *thought* is taken to mean just thinking and reasoning, Henry's outburst becomes inexplicable to the historian. Understood in its narrow sense, Collingwood's thesis would make many important historical events unintelligible to the historian since they could not be rethought in the most literal and narrow sense of the word. For this reason, many interpreters

sympathetic to Collingwood suggest that his view be
extended to include unconscious thoughts and such
nonrational dimensions of human experience as
feelings and emotions.* And so British philosopher
W. H. Walsh suggests that the historian "is interested
not solely in ideas proper, but also in the background
of feeling and emotion which those ideas had."[27]

The second and more serious weakness of Collingwood's position concerned his claim that the historian's knowledge of the thought behind past actions
must be direct and immediate.† As Walsh says, "To
say that historians must penetrate behind the phenomena they study is one thing; to hold that such penetra-
tion is achieved by an intuitive act is something very
different."[28] For this reason, Walsh concludes that
Collingwood's position cannot stand up under careful
scrutiny.

> It is not true that we grasp and understand the thought of
> past persons in a single act of intuitive insight. We have
> to discover what they were thinking, and find out why
> they thought it, by interpreting the evidence before us,
> and this process of interpretation is one in which we
> make at least implicit reference to general truths. The
> historian certainly has to do something different from the
> scientist, but he has no special powers of insight to help
> him carry out the task. He needs imagination in a large
> degree, but he needs experience too.[29]

To whatever extent Collingwood's original position
entails the notion that the thoughts of historical agents
must be apprehended immediately and that those
thoughts must be exactly like our own thoughts, his
view must be rejected. Collingwood's call to "rethink
the past" must give proper place to inference and
deduction. One possible model that would include

---

*This was how Dilthey viewed the matter. Dilthey would not
have agreed that history is concerned only with thinking or reasoning. He understood human consciousness to include the nonrational
side of man as well as reason.

†Dilthey can also be faulted on this point. He too suggested that
the operation of *Verstehen* is immediate rather than inferential in
the sense that we can pass directly from our awareness of some
expression to an understanding of what it expresses. It is difficult,
on Dilthey's analysis, to explain the many times we are mistaken
about people's inner states.

this suggestion is the kind of thinking found in detective work. Once the problem is identified (Who committed the crime?), as much evidence as possible is gathered. Then various hypotheses are tested in light of the evidence.

At the end of this chapter we will return to the topic of how contemporary idealists have revised Collingwood's theory of history. In order to maintain the connection of our argument, it is necessary now to see the influence that the idealist approach, especially the work of Collingwood, has had on Christian theologians.

Idealism and Christian Historiography

Theologian Norman Sykes calls Collingwood's distinction between the inside and the outside of historical events "the *Magna Carta* of the historian, and more particularly of the historian of the origins of Christianity."[30] As Sykes sees it, once the historian accepts the validity of Collingwood's general position, he is no longer concerned to search for facts apart from an interpretation of the facts.

> For if the secular historian is interested in Caesar's crossing of the Rubicon only in relation to the defiance of Republican law, or in the spilling of his blood in the senate house only in relation to the clash of constitutional policy between himself and his assassins, the historian of Christianity must be interested in the trial and crucifixion of Jesus in relation to the claim to Messiahship which the evangelists advance as the cause of that episode, and which they affirm to have been made by Jesus himself and rejected by the leaders of Judaism. . . . From the standpoint of historiography therefore it is no objection to the alleged historical character of the gospel tradition that it continuously blends interpretation with fact, and places the story of the public ministry, teaching, and death of Jesus within the framework of a belief in his Messiahship, vouchsafed by vision at his baptism, interpreted by a selected series of his acts and sayings, and culminating in his execution as a Messianic pretender.[31]

Collingwood and the other idealists have done the student of Christianity a service by offering an alternative to the misguided nineteenth-century attempt to divorce "fact" from interpretation. This positivist, "scientific" position led to the erroneous attempt of some Christian thinkers to separate the religion *of* Jesus from the biblical writers' religion *about* Jesus.

Also of value is the recognition that the historian is not simply concerned to discover what happened in the bare external events but that he must attempt to recover the inner thought life behind the event. As British biblical scholar William Manson writes, "To history belongs not the suffering of Jesus only, but the mind with which he approached that suffering and the interpretation which he put upon it."[32]

The idealists were also correct, as T. A. Roberts points out, in recognizing that "since historians study not mere events occurring in nature but events which are the outcome of the purposeful intentions of human beings, the historical method correspondingly demands a special technique, not required in the natural sciences, to penetrate the inside of events, thus detecting the thought they express."[33] The historian does this, as we have seen, by rethinking the past. For Collingwood, "historical activity produces accounts of past events plus their interpretation."[34]

However, there was another consequence of the idealist view of history that is more troubling for Christian historiography. Christian existentialists joined hands with the idealists in rejecting the positivist view of history. *But in doing so, the existentialists tended to turn away from the objective events of history and turn inward to an existentialist stress on subjective decision and commitment.* It is one thing to realize that there is an inner world in addition to the external events. But it is something quite different to *exalt* that inner world to the point that it *takes precedence* over the historical event and in fact makes the external event irrelevant. Later on, we will explore the existentialist turn away from history as illustrated in the position of Rudolf Bultmann. Before we close this discussion, however, it is important that we look further at how several *contemporary* philosophers of history have extended the idealist thesis in the development of a more plausible theory of historical explanation. It appears obvious that as historians and theologians seek to understand and explain such early Christian phenomena as the resurrection, they can make good use of these insights.

Further Comments on Historical Explanation

W. H. Walsh and William Dray (a British and a Canadian philosopher respectively) have offered theories of historical explanation that hold some promise for the work of all historians and theologians. In an important sense, both positions are extensions of suggestions found originally in Collingwood. Walsh points out that the Old Idealism (the idealism of Dilthey and Collingwood) rejected any place for general truths in historical explanation. Walsh thinks this was a mistake. General truths do operate in historical understanding and explanation. But this does not require a return to positivism. According to Walsh, the historian explains by simply collecting as much data about past events as possible and then locating those events in their historical context. In Walsh's theory, historical events may be viewed as rational in two quite distinct ways. Some events are rational in the sense that what happened occurred deliberately, as part of a designed plan or policy. In this sense, the crucifixion of Jesus took place because it was the deliberate goal of some. But many historical events that are not the result of intended acts may be rational in a second way: unintended acts or events may be viewed as rational when seen as part of a larger whole. In this second kind of case, the historian imposes "reason" on the events by grouping them into a trend or development. And so, many otherwise unrelated events can be linked together to make a development like the Reformation. Hence the historian can explain either becaue he finds reason (intention, purpose, goals) present within the act or because he imposes a rational structure upon a group of events. In other words, the historian tries to tie things together under some organizing concept. He attempts to show that events not previously seen as related are parts of some larger whole.

William Dray has advocated a position similar to Walsh's in an article entitled "Explaining What."[35] As Dray explained the historian's task, the historian should not try to explain *why* something happened, he should concentrate instead on explaining *what* happened. Historical explanation is, in other words, really historical interpretation. The historian explains by synthesizing the parts into a new whole, that is, by explaining what, in the context of other occurrences, the event really was. In this approach to historical explanation, the historian explains by filling in the gaps or by tracing connections between events.

According to Dray, understanding the past does not require an immediate apprehension of the precise thoughts of the people who acted in the past. Rather, we understand the past when we can put ourselves in the position of agents in the past and see how the action made sense from their perspective. Was Henry II's tirade against Thomas Becket a rational act? Probably not. But it is possible for the historian to imagine what it was like for that frustrated, enraged, and drunken king to rail against the former ally who had become his greatest enemy. In trying to understand why the historical agent did what he did, we try to get more information, and we do this by filling in more and more of the gaps. As we come to know more and more about the past, what people did in the past becomes more understandable in the sense that we can more easily see how their action was a reasonable thing for them to do, given their beliefs, feelings, and circumstances.*

Why did Pontius Pilate seek first to release Jesus and then finally turn him over to be crucified? An adequate explanation of Pilate's actions requires that we rethink his thoughts. But since we have opted for the broad interpretation of Collingwood's thesis, we must consider Pilate's relevant nonrational states as well. Following the suggestion of Walsh, under-

---

*I am intentionally omitting a great deal of the contemporary discussion about historical explanation, especially what has been called "the covering law model of historical explanation" and attempted revisions of it. While that material is extremely important for an understanding of the critical philosophy of history, much of it has only marginal relevance for the concerns of this book. The rest of the story can be gleaned by consulting chapter twelve of Nash, *Ideas of History,* volume 2, and the accompanying bibliography.

standing Pilate's actions requires that we obtain as much information as possible about him and the setting in which he acted. Perhaps at first he believed Jesus was innocent. Or perhaps he simply didn't care about the internal squabbles over Jewish belief. Perhaps he just wanted to irritate the Jewish leaders by frustrating their obvious desire to eliminate Jesus. As difficult as it may be to pin down Pilate's precise reasons for wishing to release Jesus, it is relatively easy to understand why he finally decided to turn Jesus over to be executed. When he heard voices threatening to report him to Caesar for treating a potential enemy of the Roman Empire kindly, other and more powerful motives took control, namely, fear for his own career and life. Given Pilate's beliefs, fears, desire, and ambition, from his point of view, his action was a reasonable thing to do.* Understanding and explaining a historical action requires attention to the agent's reasons for acting within the context of the full set of circumstances, real and imagined, that surround the action. Where incomplete knowledge hinders our seeing how the historical action was reasonable, the action will remain largely unintelligible. Walsh elaborates this point:

> Because the primary concern of historians is with the actions of human beings, questions about purposes, intentions, policies, ends are naturally uppermost in their minds. What might be described as the historian's standard move in seeking to understand a puzzling series of events is to reconstruct the thoughts of the agents concerned. Discovering the thought behind an action not only renders it intelligible in itself, but further serves to link it intrinsically with other actions which embody the same idea; a fact which illuminates the common histori-

---

*The statement that Pilate's act was the reasonable thing to do must not be misunderstood. Obviously, if he had fully understood who Jesus was and what he (Pilate) was doing, his action was not reasonable. We are discussing a technical point in the critical philosophy of history regarding what is required for a historian to understand and explain a historical action. Dray's position is that we can understand such an action when our knowledge about the context in which the action occurred is complete enough for us to see that, from the agent's perspective, what he did made sense— that is, it was reasonable.

cal procedure of explaining an event by locating it in its context, showing that it fits in with earlier and later events as part of the carrying out of a deliberate policy ("The Reform Movement") or, failing that, of a recognizable trend or development ("The Evolution of Parliament"). But before you can reconstruct what a man thought on a given occasion you have to specify the situation in which he was and the state of mind in which he approached it; and here reference must be made to the forces acting on him (coming out in such facts as that he was ill or tired or being blackmailed) and also to permanent features of his character (as that he was by nature rash or excessively sanguine or easily irritated).[36]

Walsh calls his theory of historical explanation *colligation,* a word that carries the idea of tying together. Colligation in history means to bring isolated observations together by some hypothesis that applies to all of them. In a sense, this is what Isaac Newton's discovery of the law of universal gravitation did. He discovered one principle that could tie together such diverse phenomena as the tides of the sea and the movements of the planets. A single hypothesis brought together hundreds of previously unrelated phenomena. So the historian seeks an explanation that will tie together a number of seemingly unrelated events of history.

William Dray's account of the same general approach is helpful:

The function of an explanation is to resolve puzzlement of some kind. When a historian sets out to explain a historical action, his problem is usually that he does not know what reason the agent had for doing it. To achieve understanding, what he seeks is information about what the agent believed to be the facts of his situation, including the likely results of taking various courses of action considered open to him, and what he wanted to accomplish: his purposes, goals, or motives. Understanding is achieved when the historian can see the reasonableness of a man's doing what this agent did, given the beliefs and purposes referred to; his action can then be explained as having been an "appropriate" one. . . . Explanation which tries to establish a connection between beliefs, motives, and actions of the indicated sort I shall call "rational explanation."[37]

A good experiment to consider in connection with the Walsh-Dray theory* of historical explanation is to imagine oneself as a history teacher about the year A.D. 2000 assigned to explain the Watergate scandal to an audience of people born after 1980. In order to explain Watergate, one would have to give as much information as possible about the agents, their state of mind, their emotions, and their beliefs. One would also have to fill in as many gaps as possible so as to provide an understanding of the context. A good historian would set the stage. He would describe how Democratic presidents prior to Nixon had done many of the same things, a fact that does not excuse Nixon but does make it possible to understand the ease with which the same kinds of actions such as taping private conversations were done. The historian would relate the national mood of hysteria and distrust over the Vietnam War, the paranoia within the White House, and so on. When sufficient information was provided to make the various actions appear as the reasonable thing to do, then and only then would the events become intelligible.

Summary

This chapter began by noting that the excesses and distortions of the historian's task contained in the positivist-scientific model of history made the kind of reaction typified in the work of Dilthey and Collingwood inevitable. But historical idealism has not been an unqualified success. It provided several important correctives to positivism by drawing attention to the important role of the historian himself in historical research. But the new emphasis on subjectivity produced its own excesses as some historians and theologians turned away from the outer, objective world of event and turned almost exclusively to the inner world of commitment and decision. The most important emphases of idealism appear to be pre-

---

*I do not wish to suggest that no differences exist between the theories of Walsh and Dray. But that would be a subject for a different kind of book. Their agreement on the essentials I have noted has produced a resourceful and fruitful theory of historical explanation.

served in the work of Neo-Idealists like Walsh and Dray whose theory of historical explanation helps us see that before the past can be understood and explained, it must first be seen as rational.

chapter four

History in the Thought of Rudolf Bultmann

The author analyzes Bultmann's disjunction of faith and history and critiques the four kinds of myths Bultmann finds in the biblical record—scientific, psychological, theological, and supernatural. He also identifies and evaluates the assumptions of form criticism.

It seems safe to say that no theologian in the twentieth century has influenced the course of Christian thinking about history, for good or ill, more than Rudolf Bultmann. A later chapter will examine his specific views about the resurrection of Jesus. The purpose of this chapter is to explore his view of the relationship between history and Christianity in general.

Born in a German Lutheran parsonage in 1884, Bultmann studied at the universities of Tübingen, Berlin, and Marburg. After teaching briefly at several universities, he returned to Marburg in 1921, where he taught until his retirement in 1951. Working

47

primarily in the area of New Testament studies, Bultmann quickly became one of the most important and most controversial Christian thinkers of the twentieth century. He died in 1976.

The key to understanding Bultmann's entire theology is recognizing that for him, Christianity should not be concerned with what happens in the objective world studied by science. Christianity should be interested primarily with what happens *within* a human being. The way Bultmann extends this conviction to history should be obvious. His brand of Christianity is not concerned with what may have happened in the *past;* it is interested chiefly in what is happening in the believer's *present* experience. Once this basic point is grasped, it will be fairly simple to understand the ease with which Bultmann minimizes the Christian's concern with history. What happened 2,000 years ago on a cross outside Jerusalem is far less important than what is taking place *now* in the existential experience of a believer. As Bultmann puts it, "Always in your present lies the meaning in history, and you cannot see it as a spectator, but only in your responsible decisions."[38] Hence Bultmann rejects any place for disinterested theoretical knowledge* in religion. Given his rejection of this, it follows that he will have little use for the kind of theoretical knowledge sought by the historian. Given his existentialist emphasis on inward commitment in the present religious experience of the believer, it follows that objective knowledge of a long-dead past will have little significance in his system.

For Bultmann, the proper foundation of Christian faith is not historical criticism but the preaching of the *kerygma,* or the Christian message. It is extremely difficult, he thinks, to reconstruct the historical foundation of the Christian faith. Any approach to Christianity via history can present only a hypothetical Jesus. The Jesus that must be presented is the Jesus who appears in the preaching of the early church. The proper object of Christian faith is not the historical

---

*An example of disinterested theoretical knowledge is a scientist's measurement of how fast a ball rolls down an incline.

Jesus but rather the historic Christ who is proclaimed in the kerygma. With regard to the historical Jesus, Bultmann's skepticism is difficult to overlook: "We can now know almost nothing concerning the life and personality of Jesus."[39] Before exploring Bultmann's analysis of faith and history further, some attention must be given to elements of his system that provide the backdrop for his particular views about history. One of the more important of these is his treatment of form and content in the Christian kerygma or message.

Form and Content
in Bultmann's
Understanding
of the
New Testament
Message

Bultmann believed that from its inception Christianity had allowed all sorts of irrelevant considerations to intrude between the message it preached and the audience to which the message was directed. The Christian kerygma came encased in a *cultural husk* that Bultmann thought could easily be discarded without affecting the *essential kernel*. In fact, the husk had to be discarded because it contained elements that distracted people from the kerygma. The most troubling aspect of this dispensable husk, for Bultmann, was its mythical character. As Bultmann put it, "The whole conception of the world which is presupposed in the preaching of Jesus as in the New Testament generally is mythological."[40] Basic to Bultmann's position, then, is the conviction that the message of the Bible remains couched in an ancient and outmoded mythology.* Bultmann's elaboration of this thesis suggests the presence of at least four different kinds of myth in the New Testament.

Bultmann's First
Type of Myth:
New Testament
Beliefs That
Contradict
Modern Science

Bultmann regards some elements of Scripture as myth because of their apparent conflict with the

---

*However, Bultmann was involved in demythologizing interpretation long before he began to call it such in the early 1940s, and it is easy to think, as Robert C. Roberts does, that labeling certain elements of the New Testament message "mythological" is little more than a convenient way of discrediting elements that ill fit an existentialist interpretation. See Roberts, *Rudolf Bultmann's Theology: A Critical Interpretation* (Grand Rapids: Eerdmans, 1976), p. 129.

teaching of natural science. The example he uses most often is the New Testament's alleged teaching of an outmoded cosmology that views the universe as existing in three separate stories: heaven, earth, and hell.[41] Bultmann's appeal to this first kind of myth is weakened by at least two considerations.

First, so far as literary records allow us to judge, human beings have often described some natural phenomena in language that was never intended to be understood literally, even in centuries when a false cosmology prevailed. When some modern person refers to the four corners of the earth, no one thinks he might be talking literally. When people refer to the sun's rising or setting, no one considers the possibility that they might actually believe that the sun rotates around the earth. These are examples of what has been termed *phenomenological language*. The phrase means that human beings frequently refer to natural phenomena as those occurrences appear to an observer on earth. The world may appear flat or it may appear that the sun comes up in the morning and sets at night. Language that refers to such phenomena (appearances) is a natural outgrowth of human observation. The appearance of similar language in the Bible may simply reflect a universal tendency to describe nature as it appears; any further inference about what the writer may have actually believed about cosmology would require much more information than the language uses that Bultmann considers. Bultmann never even begins to offer that additional evidence. In order to turn such biblical references into anything like the kind of mythology that Bultmann finds so embarrassing, he must first interpret them as literal teachings about the nature of the solar system.

Bultmann acknowledges that the language he considers mythological when it appears in the Bible frequently shows up in modern discourse. "Particularly in our day and generation, although we no longer think mythologically, we often speak of demonic powers which rule history, corrupting political and social life."[42] Since Bultmann has too high a regard for the knowledge of modern man to allow such contemporary expressions to be myth, he rescues them from the

category of myth by treating them as metaphors:
"Such language [in modern writings and speech] is
metaphorical, a figure of speech, but in it is expressed
the knowledge, the insight that the evil for which every
man is responsible individually has nevertheless become a power which mysteriously enslaves every
member of the human race."[43] This is very interesting.
When a given expression appears in the Bible, it is
myth; but when it appears in some contemporary writing, it is metaphor. Since Bultmann does not provide
any criterion to show when a particular usage of language is either mythical or metaphorical, the obvious
inference is that language is mythical when Bultmann
says it is. He begs a big question at this point. Surely
the writers of the Bible were able to refer to natural
phenomena in a metaphorical way.

Second, Bultmann's claim that biblical statements
that appear to conflict with modern science are mythical is open to a different line of criticism. It is not at
all clear what Bultmann means by "science." Consider the following claim from Bultmann's *Jesus
Christ and Mythology:* "This conception of the world
we call mythological because it is different from the
conception of the world which has been formed and
developed by science since its inception in ancient
Greece and which has been accepted by all modern
men."[44] Taken at face value, this statement suggests
an absolutization of the one particular stage of scientific thinking that happens to coincide with the
latest stage known to Bultmann.

No particular stage of science can be regarded as
stating the final truth about anything. If anything is
true about the history of science, it is the constantly
changing state of scientific knowledge. To maintain
that one particular world view is mythological because it conflicts with what science teaches at a particular stage in its development is rash, to say the
least. Bultmann attempted to evade this challenge by
admitting the constantly changing character of science, thus implying his opposition to the absolutization of any one stage in the history of scientific
thought. He wrote, "The science of today is no longer
the same as it was in the nineteenth century, and to be

sure, all the results of science are relative, and no world view of yesterday or today or tomorrow is definitive.''[45] One might think that this admission would undermine much of Bultmann's appeal to science. But he goes on to explain:

> The main point, however, is not the concrete results of scientific research and the contents of a world-view, but the method of thinking from which world-views follow. For example, it makes no difference in principle whether the earth rotates round the sun or the sun rotates round the earth, but it does make a decisive difference that modern man understands the motion of the universe as a motion which obeys a cosmic law, a law of nature which human reason can discover. Therefore, modern man acknowledges as reality only such phenomena or events as are comprehensible within the framework of the rational order of the universe.[46]

Bultmann certainly appears to be contradicting himself. On the one hand, the biblical "science" he regards as mythological is rejected because of its *content,* because its picture of the universe is in obvious conflict with the contemporary understanding of the world. But when challenged that such a position in effect absolutizes a particular stage of scientific thought, Bultmann changes ground and maintains that what he really means by science is its *method.* According to his second position, the particular model of the solar system that may appear in a document like the Bible is irrelevant; what is relevant is the *method* by which the model is arrived at and the method that counts includes the conviction that the universe operates according to laws of nature that man can discover. Taken literally, Bultmann seems to say he would have no problem with the world view of the biblical writers if they had grounded their model on the conviction that the universe was lawlike. That is, Bultmann suggests, it is not the content of the science of the biblical writers but their method that he finds troubling. But this implies that he would have been happy with any biblical cosmology if only the writers had viewed the universe as the product of natural law.

One of the sternest attacks on Bultmann's use of the word *science* appears in the work of existentialist philosopher Karl Jaspers, who thought Bultmann wavered between two different senses of the word. Sometimes, Jaspers suggested, Bultmann seems to use "science" to mean "a certain mode of thinking that is overwhelmingly current today and that is the distinguishing characteristic of modern man."[47] But understanding science in this way could not help Bultmann's argument, Jaspers pointed out. For one thing, the resurrection of Christ was regarded as impossible in the first century just as it is by modern man. Materialism and naturalism are not exclusive dispositions of twentieth-century man. Moreover, Jaspers continued, modern man has more than his share of absurd beliefs: astrology and theosophy being just two examples. Thus, belief in the supernatural did not end with the first century nor did belief in absurdities end with the rise of modern science.

As a second possible meaning of "science" in Bultmann's writings, Jaspers suggested that Bultmann may use the term to mean the modern science that began with the Renaissance and advanced so rapidly after the beginning of the eighteenth century. But, Jaspers pointed out, comparatively few modern people know very much about this science. Indeed, Jaspers wrote with biting irony, "There are many scholars, and Bultmann, a serious historian, is apparently one of them, who are unfamiliar with its principles."[48]

So, in Bultmann's search for the Christian kerygma —the *kernel* or essential message of the New Testament—he attempted to discard the cultural *husk* in which that kernel came encased. This effort he called *demythologizing*, and the first myth he tried to discard was certain elements of Scripture that conflicted with modern naturalistic science. But Bultmann did not stop with science, he also regarded many biblical statements as psychological myths.

Bultmann's Second Type of Myth: Expressions in Conflict With Modern Psychology

Bultmann also treats as myth biblical statements that, when interpreted literally, appear to conflict with modern psychology. His prime examples here are biblical references to demons and devils.[49] For example, the Gospels report that Jesus explained *some* abnormal human behavior in terms of demon possession.* While it is not clear that biblical references to natural phenomena require us to conclude that the Bible actually teaches and endorses an outmoded cosmology, there can be no question but that the Gospels teach that Jesus explained *some* instances of abnormal human behavior in terms of demon possession (Mark 5:1–20).

Bultmann obviously found the existence of demons incredible. While this may be an interesting bit of psychological information about Bultmann, it does not follow from Bultmann's or anyone else's *disbelief* that demons do not exist. It is obvious that many contemporary humans (including many who are not Christians) find belief in malevolent superhuman spirits plausible.† Bultmann's dismissal of biblical accounts of such spirits as myth appears to beg some rather basic questions.

Bultmann's Third Type of Myth: Traditional Christian Dogmas

Many people who know of Bultmann's denigration of biblical myth are unaware of the radical lengths to which he took his doctrine. Bultmann branded as myth practically every distinctive belief of traditional Christianity: the incarnation, the virgin birth, the vicarious atonement, the resurrection, the ascension, and the second coming. It is at this point that many who might have been willing to follow Bultmann's rather ambiguous lead with respect to the first two kinds of myth begin to balk. After all, what Bultmann wishes to dispose of in this third category of myth is what most traditional Catholics and Protestants regard as essential elements of the Christian religion. A religion without the incarnate, crucified, and risen Son of God may be a plausible faith, but it certainly is not the

---

*It is important to notice also that Jesus never explained all abnormal human behavior in terms of demon possession. He recognized that some instances of physical and mental illness had natural causes.

†Naturally, I do not regard the *belief in* demons as evidence for their existence any more than I view Bultmann's disbelief as proof that they do not. I am simply pointing out the ease with which Bultmann settled matters by appealing to his own intuitions.

Christian religion. What Bultmann dismisses as myth in this third category constitutes the unique foundation of historic Christianity. If these foundations are removed, Christianity is altered so dramatically that it becomes a totally new religion.

If someone were to come out with a new soft drink and call it Coca Cola, he would be sued for stealing a trademark. But this is precisely the sort of thing that theological liberals have been doing for generations. They have taken the old labels and applied them illegitimately to an entirely new product. The religion they set forth is different in every essential way from the historic Christian faith. But for some reason, they lack the integrity to give their new religion a new name. They want the advantages that the old name has built up over the centuries. Bultmann's radical redefinition of Christianity could be compared to the Reverend Jerry Falwell's starting a Baptist church in Jerusalem and calling it the Liberty Jewish Temple. In some areas of life, names do make a difference. The Christian faith has suffered immeasurable harm because of the tendency of people to use the word *Christian* in a careless and nonhistoric way. My argument would not preclude theologians like Bultmann from developing or practicing any religion they like. But when a person promotes a religion in total conflict with traditional Christianity, he ought to give it a new name that will indicate to the uninitiated that he is promoting a new product.

Bultmann's Fourth Type of Myth: Divine Intervention in the World

Bultmann finally rejects as myth the fundamental theistic conviction that a supernatural being like God can intervene in the world of space and time.[50] The only support Bultmann offers for this claim is the simple observation that "modern science does not believe that the course of nature can be interrupted or, so to speak, perforated, by supernatural powers."[51]

Mythology expresses a certain understanding of human existence. It believes that the world and human life have their ground and their limits in a power which is beyond all that we can calculate or control. Mythology speaks about this power inadequately and insufficiently because it speaks about it as if it were a worldly power. It speaks of gods who represent the power beyond the visible, comprehensible world. It speaks of gods as if they were men and of their actions as human actions, although it conceives of the gods as endowed with superhuman power and of their actions as incalculable, as capable of breaking the normal, ordinary order of events.[52]

Bultmann is attacking a straw man. The simple truth is that Bultmann is a naturalist. He believes the world is a closed system not open to intervention from any forces from outside the system. His basic world view is not that of the traditional theist who sees the world as the creation of a sovereign God and the universe as an open system. Nature is, for Bultmann, an ultimate that Bultmann's god is powerless to affect.

Notice how Bultmann's meaning of ''myth'' has become extended. A myth is no longer just an *outmoded belief* about the structure of the solar system or the cause of abnormal human behavior. *The sphere of myth now includes any acceptance of supernaturalism.*

> The historical method includes the presuppositions that history is a unity in the sense of a closed continuum of effects in which individual events are connected by the succession of cause and effect . . . the whole historical process [must be understood] as a closed unity. This closedness means that the continuum of historical happenings cannot be rent by the interference of supernatural powers and that therefore there is no ''miracle'' in this sense of the word. Such a miracle would be an event whose cause did not lie within history.[53]

Scottish theologian Thomas Torrance has criticized Bultmann's naturalism on the ground that it brings ''to the task of biblical interpretation an essentially closed mind which can only result in some sort of scientific or sociological reductionism.''[54]

A major irony attaches to Bultmann's refusal to allow the possibility that the transcendent God can intervene in the physical universe. It is well known that Bultmann criticized certain features of early Christianity for what he took to be its undue dependence on Gnosticism. But the irony is that Bultmann's exaggerated stress on the divine transcendence that rules out any possibility of God's having contact with the physical world turns out to be a capitulation to a major gnostic doctrine. The Gnostics so exaggerated the *otherness* of God in contrast to the material world that they ruled out any direct contact between God and the world. This is effectively what Bultmann did. This does not mean that Bultmann accepted the entire gnostic system. In fact, he regarded himself as a critic of what he saw as gnostic tendencies in early Christianity, such as the belief that a supernatural Jesus from ''out there'' enters this world to redeem man. But what was most central in Gnosticism was the utter disparity between the divine Spirit and corrupt matter, the exclusive separation between God and the world. Bultmann, the avowed enemy of gnostic tendencies in Christianity, turns out to be the real gnostic.

Bultmann's Program of Demythologization

Despite the problems that Bultmann perceives in the mythical element of Scripture, he believes the message of salvation comes couched in mythological language. To the extent that modern man regards that mythical component as essential to the message, he will view the message with suspicion or disdain. Such an attitude, says Bultmann, confuses the husk with the kernel of the New Testament message. Bultmann still contends that modern man should not reject the message because of the mythical form in which it comes. Rather, he should strip away the husk and get down to the kernel. He should distinguish the *content* of the message from the *form* in which it may come. The form of the message includes all the mythological baggage that Bultmann believes accompanies the message. The content of the message is the kerygma, the preaching of the early church. What is required is that this outmoded form be reinterpreted so that modern man may see what is really crucial and central to the biblical message. As Oxford professor John Macquarrie explains:

If Christianity is inextricably bound up with the outworn mythology and cosmology of the first century of our era, then it would seem that unless we are prepared to make a sacrifice of the intellect, we must reluctantly say good-by to the Christian faith, as so many moderns have felt themselves compelled to do when confronted by the bewildering and unintelligible ideas of the New Testament.

Bultmann himself, however, when confronted with this situation, does not say good-by to Christianity. He believes that hidden in the mythical language of the New Testament lies a supreme truth—nothing less than God's word addressed to man. He is concerned that we in the modern world should hear this word and respond to it.[55]

What does Bultmann mean by *demythologization?* In one place, he explains, "To de-mythologize is to deny that the message of Scripture and of the Church is bound to an ancient world-view which is obsolete."[56] But if this were all that Bultmann meant by his call to demythologize the Bible, even his most outspoken critics on the theological right would be Bultmannians. None of them believes the world is flat or that the Bible *teaches* a flat earth. Theological conservatives are eager to show that the message of the Bible is not tied to an obsolete view of the world. In another place, Bultmann writes, *"Demythologization is an hermeneutic method,* that is to say, a method of interpretation and exegesis."[57] In other words, demythologization is a process of retranslating the message of the Bible into language and concepts that modern man can understand and accept. Demythologization is translating done with an apologetic concern that leads to more effective proclamation. Bultmann believes that he and his followers are able to preach the Word in more contemporary language and thus make it more understandable and acceptable to modern man.

But as we have seen, the myths that Bultmann wishes to strip away from the kernel of the Christian message turn out to include features that traditional Christianity has regarded as an essential part of that kernel. It is clear that, at least in Bultmann's hands, demythologization is not a neutral method of interpretation. It is a method used by a group of thinkers who have decided before the fact what is essential and what is nonessential to the Christian message.

Bultmann's demythologization of the New Testament led him to a theology that he admitted was highly reminiscent of themes found in the early work of the German existentialist Martin Heidegger. Bultmann disavows any dependence on Heidegger, claiming instead only that he saw in Heidegger's philosophy some of the same existential themes he found in the New Testament. Even though his retranslation of the New Testament was based on a conceptual framework borrowed from Heidegger, Bultmann insists that the message of the kerygma as he understands it would have been the same even if Heidegger had never been born. For Bultmann, the goal of the New Testament is human self-understanding. When done properly, demythologization of the New Testament will tell us what it means for a human being to exist.* According to Bultmann's existential reinterpretation of the New Testament, man does not need salvation from sin so much as he needs salvation from himself. The attainment of existential self-awareness does not depend on Jesus' dying on a cross or rising from the dead. Instead of attempting to bring people to a reconciliation with a holy God through the sacrifice of Christ, the existentialist seeks to bring them to a self-awareness in which one lays himself open to the future with its possibilities of genuine existence.

Bultmann's Theology and Heidegger's Philosophy

As we have seen, Bultmann believes that Christianity need not be concerned with what happens in the objective world studied by science; what is important is what takes place within a human being. Similarly, Christianity is not especially concerned with what may have happened in the *past;* its primary interest is in what is happening in the believer's *pres-*

Bultmann's View of History

---

*A discussion of specific details of Heidegger's philosophy and Bultmann's use of them would take us too far from our subject. But for a clear and jargon-free presentation of the basic Heideggerian idea, see chapter 1 of Roberts, *Rudolf Bultmann's Theology*. Roberts summarizes the Heideggerian metaphysic as "the existence/world dichotomy" and expounds it in five connections: "world" as the controllable, as physical nature, as general truth, as the past, and as personality.

ent experience. The real value of the New Testament kerygma is not derived from what happened 2,000 years ago. That is unimportant. The real value and meaning of Christianity lies in what it means to me today. "Always in your present lies the meaning in history, and you cannot see it as a spectator, but only in your responsible decisions."[58]

Bultmann has at least three reasons for disjoining faith and history. The first is an apologetic concern to make the Christian faith palatable to modern man. Too many events in the alleged history of Jesus are theoretically impossible and thus incredible to modern man. Claims that Jesus walked on water or turned water into wine or cast out demons or fed five thousand people with a couple of fish and five loaves of bread do more harm than good, Bultmann believes. He thinks attempts to make such events an integral part of the kerygma will only succeed in turning off modern people who no longer believe in the possibility of such miracles. If such nonessential elements are stripped from the kerygma, it becomes easier for people today to accept what is truly essential in the kerygma.

Bultmann's second reason for separating faith and history is his conviction that the gospel is too important to be grounded on anything as unreliable, uncertain, and subject to change as history. The results of historical research can never be certain. Therefore, resting anything as important as the gospel on history is to do the kerygma a disservice. As American New Testament scholar Norman Perrin* explains, "[F]aith as such is necessarily independent of historical facts, even historical facts about Jesus. In practice, today's assured historical facts tend to become tomorrow's abandoned historian's hypotheses. . . ."[59]

Third, Bultmann grounds his distrust of *Historie* on a surprising appeal to the Pauline and Lutheran doctrine of justification by faith. Just as the apostle Paul and Martin Luther, prior to their conversions, had sought security in things, many other Christians seek security for their faith in history. Bultmann believes

---

*Perrin, now deceased, was a leading Bultmannian.

that the doctrine of justification by faith means letting go of history as well as letting go of good works. Bultmann believes that many Christians are inconsistent in the sense that though they profess belief in justification by faith in their soteriology, they practice a doctrine of works in epistemology. In Bultmann's words:

> Our radical attempt to demythologize the New Testament is in fact a perfect parallel to St. Paul's and Luther's doctrine of justification by faith alone apart from the works of the law. Or rather, it carries this doctrine to its logical conclusion in the field of epistemology. Like the doctrine of justification it destroys every false security and every false demand for it on the part of man, whether he sees it in his good works or in his ascertainable knowledge. The man who wishes to believe in God as his God must realize that he has nothing in his hand on which to base his faith. He is suspended in mid-air, and cannot demand a proof of the Word which addresses him. For the ground and object of faith are identical. Security can be found only by abandoning all security, by being ready, as Luther put it, to plunge into the inner darkness. Faith in God means faith in justification.[60]

Bultmann's comparison of his method to the Pauline and Lutheran doctrine of justification by faith is sincere but mistaken. As British philosopher Basil Mitchell complains:

> There is not in point of fact any warrant in logic for proceeding from the theological doctrine of justification by faith alone to the epistemological doctrine that faith admits of no rational support. The former insists that man cannot earn salvation by good works and is a part of the teaching of traditional Christian theism . . . the latter claims that traditional Christian theism, of which this theological doctrine is a part, must be accepted without question by an existential choice for which no reason can or need be given. They are entirely distinct and it is an evident *non sequitur* to suppose that the one follows from the other.[61]

Bultmann's elimination of knowledge as a ground of faith does not really stem from Paul via Martin Luther. It comes straight from the philosophy of Immanuel Kant. Modern theology since Kant has been infected by a faulty epistemology that teaches that faith and theoretical knowledge have absolutely nothing in common. Bultmann is captive to this epistemology that has been the legacy of too much Protestant theology since Kant, a legacy that exaggerates the differences between faith and knowledge.*

Genuine faith does not exist in a cognitive vacuum. In everyday life, we proportion faith and trust to the evidences. In ordinary, everyday experience, the person who believes is most deserving of respect when his belief is supported by reasons. *Believing against reason is credulity, not faith.*

Theologian I. Howard Marshall sums up Bultmann's existentialist approach to faith and history:

> The function of the Bible is to bring man to self-awareness and thus to save him by setting him free from himself. No act of God is needed to save men in the sense that some historical event (such as the cross) is a means of setting him free from sin. But when the Christian message about the cross comes to men, it enables man to see himself, to acknowledge the poverty of his existence, and to lay himself open to the future with its possibility of genuine existence. Such a message is almost completely independent of history, and needs no historical proof or historical backing. On this view, the traditional concept of God is a mythological survival from the past; when demythologised and restated in modern terms, it conveys the existentialist message. Even Jesus himself is scarcely necessary, although the fact of Jesus as the One through whom man comes to self-awareness is strenuously defended.[62]†

---

*The story of this legacy is detailed in Ronald Nash, *The Word of God and the Mind of Man* (Grand Rapids: Zondervan, 1982).

†Roberts *(Rudolf Bultmann's Theology,* pp. 100ff.) offers an explanation of Bultmann's strangely strenuous assertion that the kerygma must make reference to the historical Jesus. He distinguishes three possible connections between the historical Jesus and the present-day kerygma. If the kerygma is a narrative about Jesus, then the connection is *logical* (the kerygma can't be the kerygma without referring to Jesus); if the kerygma was historically set in motion by Jesus, then the connection is *genetic;* and if the kerygma causes self-transcendence in modern-day believers just as Jesus caused it in his disciples, then the connection is *analogical.* Roberts shows that where Bultmann makes this strenuous assertion, it is, by and large, the genetic and analogical connections that he is referring to, and not the logical one. However, only the logical connection can make reference to Jesus a necessary constituent of the kerygma.

Bultmann's writings make clear his indebtedness to historical idealists like Dilthey and Collingwood. From Dilthey, Bultmann learned that "the interpreter must reexperience the original creative moment in which an author gave expression to life."[63] From Collingwood, Bultmann drew the notion that the historian must relive the past in his own present experience.

> The meaning in history lies always in the present, and when the present is conceived as the eschatological present by Christian faith, the meaning in history is realized. Anyone who complains: "I cannot see meaning in history, and therefore my life, which is interwoven in history, is meaningless," is to be admonished: "Do not look around yourself into universal history, you must look into your own personal history. Always in your present lies the meaning in history. . . . In every moment slumbers the possibility of being the eschatological moment. You must awaken it.[64]

In another book, Bultmann discusses our grasp of history in terms clearly reminiscent of Dilthey's distinction between the natural and the human sciences:

> The essence of history cannot be grasped by "viewing" it, as we view our natural environment. . . . Our relationship to history is wholly different from our relationship to nature. . . . When [a human being] observes nature, he perceives there something objective which is not himself. When he turns his attention to history, however, he must admit himself to be part of history. . . . He cannot observe this [living] complex [of events] objectively as he can observe natural phenomena. . . . Hence there cannot be impersonal observation of nature.[65]

During the long and heated debate over Bultmann's theology, post-Bultmannian theology came to view Bultmann's radical disjunction between faith and history as the Achilles heel of his system. While the major theologians after Bultmann often disagree as to how his challenge should be met and his errors corrected, they agree that Bultmann's radical separation of *Historie* from *Geschichte* must be abandoned. The essence of the conservative rejection of Bultmann is expressed by American theologian Kenneth Kantzer:

Bultmann, who denies the objective reality of the divine-human Christ and relegates the mighty acts of God to mythologized insights into the meaning of authentic human existence, is not really *interpreting* the teaching of the New Testament; he is rather *eliminating* the teaching of the New Testament. We agree with Barth, against Bultmann, that the heart of biblical Christianity is what God did objectively in history as He from His eternity took time to become man, to die on the cross, and to rise again from the dead on the third day in order to redeem man to himself.[66]

Bultmann proudly informed the world that he had demythologized Christianity in an effort to make paramount the kerygma of the early church. Unfortunately, and this is something Bultmann himself never realized, he also dehistoricized and dekerygmatized Christianity. Bultmann sincerely believed he was serving the Christian faith by making the Christian message more intelligible and acceptable to modern man. It is obvious that what Bultmann regarded as a defense of the Christian religion involved entirely too many concessions to contemporary unbelief—his own world view was a form of naturalism—and thus resulted in his transforming historic Christianity into what amounted to a new and different religion.

Bultmann and Form Criticism

One final feature of Bultmann's thought remains to be discussed in this chapter.* Bultmann has been a major influence on the important twentiety-century biblical method known as form criticism. Form criticism offered a new way of reading the Gospels that helped discredit the methodology behind the liberal quest for the historical Jesus and helped set the tone for a new approach to questions about the relationship between history and the Christian faith.

According to form criticism, the Gospels were not simply historical narratives about Jesus. They were the end result of a long process of oral tradition that

---

*We will return to the topic of Bultmann's view of history in chapter 7—on the resurrection of Christ.

had been collected, preserved, and edited.* Primitive Christianity first passed on its memories and traditions about Jesus' life and teaching orally. Gradually this became a kind of oral tradition that assumed different forms (pronouncement stories, miracle stories, paradigms, etc.). As time passed, some of these sayings were lost. But others came to be valued for their practical importance in solving problems that began to develop in the church. As the form critic saw it, the traditions about Jesus that survived did so because a particular life situation *(Sitz im Leben)* in the early church provided a reason for its preservation. For example, the form critic suggests, the story of Jesus picking grain for food on the Sabbath was preserved because of its relevance for a problem within the early church about Sabbath observance. The Gospels were viewed by form critics as the product of a long and complex process by which an original collection of oral traditions came to be preserved because of their practical relevance for the church at a time some distance removed from eyewitness testimony. Emphasis was given to the role of the Gospels as interpretations of Jesus' life and teaching. Deemphasized was the earlier search for objective, dispassionate eyewitness reports about what Jesus did and taught. For the form critic, then, the Gospels were an important source of information about what the church believed about Jesus at the time the Gospels were formulated. The extent to which the Gospels were also reliable sources of information about the historical Jesus became a question to which form critics gave different, often conflicting, answers.†

---

*Radical form critics believe that the church not only preserved and passed on the tradition about Jesus but actually created or reshaped that tradition.

†Other features of the form-critical position are passed over because they are of less importance for our purposes. Form critics wished to discover, if possible, the earliest form of a tradition and explain any changes it may have undergone. Frequently, this concern was combined with the belief that the particular form a tradition was believed to have at an earlier stage was a clue to its historical reliability. The clue to these changes in the tradition lay, form critics thought, in the kind of church situation in which the stories were being circulated.

Many critics of form criticism fail to distinguish between the *neutral method* of form criticism, which can be useful in a number of ways to an understanding of Scripture, and the *presuppositions* that some form critics insist on bringing to their use of the method. Several positive contributions of form criticism stand out. For one thing, its stress on a period of oral tradition prior to the writing of the Gospels countered an earlier emphasis on exclusively written sources for the Gospels. In its attempt to get behind the written sources, form criticism sought to move beyond the problems inherent in the earlier stress on written sources. Form criticism also drew important attention to the fact that the community of the early church had a practical interest in the tradition it transmitted. Form criticism helped clarify ways in which the practical concerns of the early Christian community shaped and preserved its memories of Jesus. Form critics were correct in noting that the Gospels were written for specific reasons. The selection and arrangement of material in the Gospels reflected practical concerns addressed by the writers.

But like most neutral methods, form criticism could also be used for destructive purposes when controlled by negative presuppositions. Critics of form criticism should be careful to note that their objections are directed not to the method itself but to the presuppositions of some adherents of the approach who sought to use it in the service of historical skepticism. Earlier theologians who had been involved in the nineteenth-century quest for the historical Jesus believed that once the Gospels were stripped of their supernatural elements, they could still be used to arrive at a historical core of information about Jesus. But some form critics used their method to undermine what little historical credibility the Gospels had left so that it became difficult, on their grounds, to get behind the Gospel material to find the real Jesus.

Rudolf Bultmann was one form critic who combined the method with an a priori skepticism about the historical Jesus. As he put it, "I do indeed think that we can now know nothing concerning the life and personality of Jesus, since early Christian sources show no interest in either, are more fragmentary and often legendary and other sources about Jesus do not exist."[67] A similar historical skepticism appeared in the writings of Bultmann's American disciple, Norman Perrin, who declared, "So far as we can tell today, there is no single pericope anywhere in the gospels, the present purpose of which is to preserve a historical reminiscence of the earthly Jesus, although there may be some which do in fact come near to doing so. . . ."[68] New Testament scholar R. H. Lightfoot summed up the miniscule amount of historical information skeptical form critics thought could be squeezed from the Gospels when he wrote, "It seems then that the form of the earthly no less than the heavenly Christ is for the most part hidden from us. For all the inestimable value of the gospels they yield us little more than a whisper of His voice; we trace in them but the outskirts of His ways."[69]

Once again I stress that by itself the form critical method does not require one to believe the early church *invented* its stories about Jesus. The method can be used by one who believes the stories were recollections of what Jesus actually did and said, recollections that came to be preserved because of their relevance for some later life situation in the church. It is unfortunate that some form critics combined their method with presuppositions that precluded any significant historical role for the text. Historian A. N. Sherwin-White has commented:

> It is astonishing that while Graeco-Roman historians have been growing in confidence, the twentieth-century study of the Gospel narratives, starting from no less promising material, has taken so gloomy a turn in the development of form-criticism that the more advanced exponents of it apparently maintain . . . that the historical Christ is unknowable and the history of his mission cannot be written.[70]

But it is not form criticism itself that is under fire here so much as it is the presuppositions that thinkers like Bultmann and Perrin brought to their use of the method. According to them, the Gospels witness primarily to the *Sitz im Leben* (life situation) of the early church and only secondarily to the historical Jesus.[71]

It is clearly consistent with the form-critical method to recognize the role that a later life situation may have had in preserving a tradition while also allowing that the tradition points to early historical events. As American theologian Charles C. Anderson points out, "The application of the sayings of Jesus to the needs of the early church does not by virtue of that fact alone take them out of the possibility of having been historical utterances of Jesus prior to his death."[72] Instead of assuming that the early church fabricated stories about Jesus to help it deal with its problems, it makes even better sense to assume that considerations about practical relevance led the church to preserve statements originally made by Jesus. D. M. Baillie, for one, complained that it seldom seemed to occur to some form critics "that the story may have been handed on simply or primarily *because it was true,* because the incident had actually taken place in the ministry of Jesus, and was therefore of great interest to his followers, even if they sometimes failed to understand it."[73]

The skeptical form criticism of thinkers like Bultmann and Perrin has been attacked on several grounds. For one thing, their position depends on the questionable assumption that the early church had little interest in the actual deeds and sayings of Jesus. In other words, the early church was more interested in the Christ of faith than with the Jesus of history. Second, the skeptics assumed that the Gospels are primarily kerygmatic or preaching documents that are unconcerned with either biography or history. As Norman Perrin worded it:

> The main purpose for the creation, the circulation, and the use of these forms was not to preserve the history of Jesus, but to strengthen the life of the church. Thus these forms reflect the concern of the church, and both the form and content have been influenced by the faith and theology of the church, as well as by her situation and practice.[74]

Elsewhere Perrin wrote, "It is the fact that the evangelists were able to use the story to serve their purposes that has caused it to be preserved, not an interest in historical reminiscence as such."[75] For those holding such a view then, the primary concern of the Gospel writers was to preach the risen Christ and not to convey historical reminiscences about the Jesus of history.

Certainly the Gospels were not written as biographies of Jesus. Nor were they historical accounts free of any theological interest and perspective. But it is surely an overstatement to claim that the Gospels contain *no* concern with biographical or historical truth.

Another questionable assumption underlying much contemporary historical skepticism about the Gospels is that the discovery of a theological motive in a Gospel necessarily involves a legitimate suspicion about the historical reliability of the material. This radical disjunction between either history or theology is apparent in the writing of Norman Perrin, who, while commenting on Luke's obvious theological interests, stated, "Luke is in no way motivated by a desire to exercise historical accuracy, but entirely by his theological concept of the role of Jerusalem in the history of salvation."[76] Left unanswered by historical skeptics is the question of why an interest in theological matters is necessarily incompatible with an interest in historical truth. "It seems to be an extremely tenaciously held misapprehension among exegetes that an early Christian author must *either* be a purposeful theologian and writer *or* a fairly reliable historian."[77] The skeptic's position here is an extension of a view called *hard relativism,* which I will criticize in a later chapter. It is the belief that it is logically impossible for the historian to free himself from the influence of his interests and his milieu. But as we will see shortly, the unavoidability of the historian's own subjectivity does not necessitate his inability to write a true historical account.

It is one thing to note that the Gospel writers selected from the material available to them and applied that material to practical uses. It is quite another to suggest that they felt no constraints against inventing new traditions if it suited some practical purpose. While the biblical writers obviously felt free to select and adapt their material, they worked under an obligation to preserve the truth about what Jesus actually did and taught. Theologian R. T. France explains:

> While it is undeniable that the evangelists and their predecessors adapted, selected, and reshaped the material which came down to them, there is no reason to extend this "freedom" to include the *creation* of new sayings attributed to Jesus' that in fact such evidence as we have points decisively the other way, to a respect for the sayings of Jesus as such which was sufficient to prevent any of his followers attributing their own teaching to him. If the Christian church did not share the rabbinic concern for verbatim transmission and reproduction of the tradition, there is every reason to believe that they did share the Jewish respect for the authoritative teaching of the Master. The sceptical assumption, repeated so often that it has become an axiom, that the early church saw no difference between what Jesus said on earth and what the risen Christ said through his church, is not only very improbable, given the milieu of Palestinian Judaism, but is contrary to such evidence as the New Testament provides.[78]

Selectivity does not entail creativity. Theological concern does not necessarily imply disinterest in historical accuracy.

In an important article published in the *Anglican Theological Review,* theologian William G. Doty drew attention to several other criticisms of the form-critical method. He pointed out that skeptical form critics fail to "take seriously enough the possibility that Jesus consciously formulated his sayings with the intention of securing them for transmission."[79] After all, any good teacher wants to assure that what he teaches will be remembered and transmitted accurately. Moreover, Doty continued, skeptical form critics play down the important role of eyewitness testimony to what Jesus said and did:

> Critics who have been dismayed by the form critics' negative historical evaluations have stoutly defended the historicity of the synoptic materials by reference to the probability that the traditions were secured for the early communities by eyewitnesses. These critics [of form

criticism] point to the possibility that first generation Christians were either still living, or had carefully passed on their first-hand experiences to the compilers of the gospels.[80]

Other critics of skeptical form criticism have faulted it for its almost exclusive preoccupation with the life situation of Christianity *after* the resurrection of Jesus. Why should the life situation of Christians involved in the public ministry of Jesus be excluded as a possible influence on the tradition? Why should a form critic restrict himself to life situations that developed *after* Easter? Skeptical form critics seem to have adopted an arbitrary starting point for their method. They have an artificial horizon in that they hesitate to go beyond the end of Jesus' earthly life and consider the possibility that there might have been life situations in the period before Easter that could have given rise to and affected the transmission of the traditions.

A pivotal issue in the debate concerns placement of the burden of proof. Some form critics such as Norman Perrin have claimed that the burden of proof must rest on those who regard the sources as authentic.[81] But as New Testament authority Joachim Jeremias asks, Why should the burden of proof not fall on the skeptic?[82] Why not presume that if anything is to be proved, it must be the *inauthenticity* of some saying of Jesus? Catholic scholar Neil McEleney points out how Jeremias's presumption accords more closely with accepted journalistic practice:

This debate over the "burden of proof" points up the importance of the criterion which I shall call "historical presumption". . . . Briefly, it is this, that one accepts a statement upon the word of the reporter unless he has reason not to do so. In other words, in the normal course of human affairs, one does not suspend judgment when told that a certain speaker has said something but presumes competence and reliability upon the part of the reporter and accepts his word unless there are reasonable grounds for denying it. Without such presumption, all histories, news reports, etc., are open to rejection, and we can have no assurance of what we do not immediately experience. This presumption, then, tips the balance in favor of the authenticity of words attributed to Jesus where no reason makes us suspect otherwise. Of course, one can be mistaken or be deceived in accepting the word of a reporter and only discover the truth later on, but this does not affect the basic principle that the presumption is in favor of veracity, and where this means assertion of authenticity, it is in favor of authenticity.[83]

As Jeremias explains his principle: "We are justified in drawing up the following principle of method: In the synoptic tradition it is the inauthenticity, and not the authenticity, of the sayings of Jesus that must be demonstrated."[84]

It is a sign of renewed health and common sense in Christian theology that many post-Bultmannians now reject the historical skepticism of Bultmann and allow that enough trustworthy material can be identified to make possible a reconstruction of a picture of Jesus. Once again, the indispensability of the historical Jesus is being recognized. But this recognition occurs in a context that is aware of all that has transpired since the collapse of the nineteenth-century quest.

**Appendix:
Redaction Criticism**

It is important to note that form criticism, the method to which Rudolf Bultmann made such an important contribution, has produced several stepchildren, including a methodology sometimes called redaction criticism *(Redaktionsgeschichte)*. While form criticism tended to concentrate on smaller independent units of material within the Gospels, redaction criticism is more interested in the Gospels as literary wholes. Instead of viewing the Gospel writers as people who simply collected and passed on material, redaction criticism acknowledges the role of the Evangelists as theological interpreters of the tradition. As Robert H. Stein observes:

> It is now generally recognized that the evangelists were not merely "scissors and paste men." On the contrary the "scissors" were manipulated by a theological hand, and the "paste" was impregnated with a particular theology. . . . It is true that [the evangelists] collected the gospel traditions and were limited by them, but each had a theological purpose in writing his gospel.[85]

Redaction criticism views the Gospel writers not just as compilers and arrangers but as theological writers.

Many redaction critics have a broader notion of the method. Norman Perrin, for example, argues that redaction criticism "is concerned with studying the theological motivation of an author as this is revealed in the collection, arrangement, editing, and modification of traditional material, and in the composition of new material or the creation of new forms within the traditions of early Christianity."[86] Stephen S. Smalley, on the other hand, has argued that a distinction be drawn between redaction criticism and what he calls composition criticism.[87] While redaction criticism "is the study of the observable changes introduced by the Gospel writers into the traditional material they received and used," composition criticism "examines the *arrangement* of this material, an arrangement which is motivated by the theological understanding and intention of the evangelists."[88]

The whole matter of an attempted contrast between redaction criticism and composition criticism is somewhat vague in current scholarship. In the view of some thinkers, composition criticism goes beyond redaction criticism by suggesting that the evangelists constructed entirely new sayings, which they then attributed to Jesus. Many conservative thinkers who find redaction criticism a useful tool regard this extension of method (composition criticism) as too radical. It is probably safe to say that most contemporary critics reject Smalley's restricted sense of redaction criticism and include within the notion of redaction criticism the notion of arrangement of and additions to the traditional material.*

Understood in its more restricted sense, redaction criticism has relevance for the debate over the Jesus of history. To whatever extent redaction criticism serves as the ground for a *new* quest for the historical Jesus, it reminds us that such a quest must include a balance between history and faith in the sense that the basic sources for the life of Jesus (the Gospels) are them-

---

*These additions are often thought to include entirely new sayings and stories.

selves a mixture of history and theology. Smalley points out that

> the method of redaction criticism is clearly of importance to this question of Christian origins. For we are bound to recognize that the Gospels were written from within a circle of faith, by those who in a particular first-century environment became convinced that Jesus of Nazareth was the Christ of God, and that he had risen from the dead. Inevitably, therefore, the evangelists reported the Jesus tradition from their own understanding, and coloured it with their own outlook.[89]

But as Smalley continues, this need not imply that the Gospel writers produced only an imaginative interpretation of Jesus with loose or even nonexistent historical ties. The radical claim that there is no connection between the Christ of faith and the Jesus of history presupposes

> that the evangelists themselves were unaware of the distinction between history and faith, and were prepared to disregard the former completely in the interests of the latter. We are not, in fact, compelled to believe that this was the case. If the Gospel writers were, on the contrary, sensitive to what was historical and what was kerygmatic (as there are real grounds for supposing), it is unlikely that they would have treated their traditional sources for the words and works of Jesus with anything but respect. All the more would respect have been shown by the evangelists, indeed, if (as is probable) eyewitnesses were still around.[90]

In other words, redaction criticism and form criticism are methods that are not necessarily incompatible with either a high view of Scripture or the conviction that the New Testament picture of Jesus is grounded on historical information. A conservative use of redaction criticism would suggest that the Evangelists started with the historical information available to them and "drew out the theological implications of the history which they recorded."[91] Starting with the apostolic tradition about Jesus, the Evangelists expressed their own theological understanding of the tradition by the arrangement of their Gospels and by the seams that tied the various units of tradition to one another.

Used with care, redaction criticism provides the student of the New Testament with a number of advantages. For one thing, it can help him see the interrelationship between faith and history in the early Christian community. The Gospel writers were not interested in recording bare facts. The Gospels reflect their writers' interaction with and theological interpretation of history. William Lane correctly notes:

> In contrast to the form-critical picture of tradition as a ball which was "somehow" fashioned, only to be tossed rather carelessly from redactor to redactor—each leaving only a very smudgy fingerprint—*Redaktionsgeschichte* restores the dimension of depth to the evangelist as a man motivated by purpose who insisted upon a Christ-related-to-our-situation theology and so succeeded in conveying a sense of immediacy throughout his Gospel.[92]

Furthermore, redaction criticism stresses the importance of studying the Gospels as wholes and not, as was so often the case with form-critical studies, as compilations of smaller independent units. Redaction criticism can help identify what the Gospel writers themselves contributed to their source material, a discovery that has obvious implications for the interpretation of the Gospels. Redaction criticism can also unveil the major reasons each Evangelist had for writing his interpretation of the traditions.

But redaction criticism also carries certain dangers that require that it be used with care. The analysis of some redaction critics is highly conjectural and hence highly subjective. Moreover, one often finds a disregard for the distinction between redaction criticism and what Smalley has called composition criticism. Redaction criticism should not imply the creation of new material. The recognition of the presence of redactional activity on the part of the Evangelists does not entail a forced choice between history and faith, between the apostolic tradition and the theological interpretation of the Evangelists.[93]

jectivity is not absence of criticism, but unreserved submission to further criticism, complete openness, withholding nothing from judgment.[94]

Is history open to constant criticism and revision? *It had better be*. If it is not, historical writing would be arbitrary, subject to every whim and caprice of the author. Understood in this first sense, historical objectivity is a necessary and desirable goal. Is history value-free? As I shall argue shortly, no. But I hasten to add that this admission by itself does not imply any radical kind of historical relativism.

The distinction I have drawn between the two meanings of historical objectivity makes it easier to see that four possible positions on this subject are available. Historical relativism comes in two forms: hard and soft relativism. Historical objectivism also assumes two forms: hard and soft objectivism.

What we call *hard relativism* in history is the view that the subjectivity of the historian is so radical and so inescapable that the discovery of any truth about the past is impossible. According to this view, no historian can ever free himself from his own subjectivity (his perspective, his values, his biases, etc.) sufficiently to discover the truth about the past. Therefore, knowledge about the past is impossible. Hard relativism, then, necessarily involves historical skepticism. According to this view, history is completely subjective, relative, and arbitrary.

Hard objectivism is my name for the position that it is possible for the historian to free himself from subjective judgments and interpretations and reach the point where he simply reports the facts. According to the hard objectivist, all subjectivity can in principle be eliminated from history, a fact that, if true, would make history a value-free inquiry.

Both hard relativism and hard objectivism approach the question of historical objectivity in the second (valuational) sense noted earlier. A hard objectivist holds that the historian can achieve independence from his interests and values and write a value-free history. Thus for him, history can be objective. A

chapter five

Can History Be Objective?

This chapter considers the four ways the question about the possibility of objectivity in history can be answered— hard and soft relativism, and hard and soft objectivism.

To what extent can the historian attain objectivity? This question is one of the most important and at the same time one of the most puzzling subjects discussed in the philosophy of history. The debate over whether the historian can achieve impartial and objective knowledge about the past has obvious relevance for Christianity. Regardless of the position taken on the question, some impact on Christian belief will be felt.

Suppose one adopts a radically *relativist position* toward history. Radical relativism is the view that impartial and objective historical knowledge about anything in the past is impossible. Since Christianity is a historical religion in the sense that the historicity of certain events like the crucifixion and the resurrection are a necessary condition for its truth, the skepticism about the past that must result from a total historical relativism would seriously weaken one of Christianity's major apologetic foundations. A thinking person can hardly embrace a radical historical relativism with any feeling of joy. If historical relativism should prove to be true, no knowledge about any event in the past would be possible.* Major alterations in the presentation and defense of Christian theism would be necessary.

But if an acceptance of a radical historical relativism would present us with problems, we will not get much relief by turning to a radical *historical objectivism*. The difficulties created by this second option are visible in the nineteenth-century debate over the nature of historical understanding. Inspired by Ranke's search for the past as it really was, many scholars assumed that an objective knowledge of the past was not only possible but mandatory. Anything less than a *complete* and *impartial account* of some event or series of events in the past was bad history. But once this assumption was made and people conceded that the New Testament Gospels were partisan interpretations of the life and teaching of Jesus, the historical veracity of those writings was called into question. If a *completely objective* history is the only acceptable norm, then the search for the historical foundations of Christianity is in trouble from the very start.

Some Christian apologists have thought it possible to use historical objectivity as one foundation for their defense of the faith. As they see it, an impartial and objective knowledge of the past is possible; the Bible provides this kind of evidence for decisive events like the resurrection; therefore, there is a *conclusive historical "proof"* for the Christian faith.† While I do not wish to minimize the importance of the historical evidences for the Christian faith, the argument must be used with a bit more care and historical acumen that is often displayed in the writings of the eviden-

tialist apologists. It seems that they are ofte
slighting serious problems and oversimplif
crucial issues. Whether this perception is
not, their method seldom impresses seriou
of history.

The problem of historical objectivity
more difficult than it really is because peo
attentive to a crucial distinction between tw
which history may be said to be objective.
on which sense of the word *objective* is
question about history's objectivity may c
answered both yes and no. The propositio
is objective'' may mean either:

1. the historian's reconstruction of
   always open to criticism and revis
2. the historian's reconstruction of th
   be value-free.

Corresponding to these two views, the clai
is not objective'' may mean either:

1. the historian's work is arbitrary*
2. the historian's work is subjective.

Much of the confusion that characteriz
about historical objectivity results from a
keep these two sets of issues distinct.

As a start toward presenting my own
affirm the view that history can be objec
sense of being open to critical revision.
pher Max Fisch put it:

> The historian is not blamed for praising and
> praised for doing neither, but blamed if ante
> ments of value blind him to contrary ev
> praised if his selection and treatment of
> clearly not unbalanced by the desire to suppo
> formed in advance of the search for eviden

---

*Of course it would also follow that no one could know whether or not relativism is true.

†Advocates of this view are sometimes called evidentialists.

---

*Two additional points by way of explanation: th
trary and *subjective* are also vague and will require f
ing as we continue. The basic point I am making is th
history is objective may mean either that the histori
necessary reflection of his own subjective interests
that the historian's work is so logically independent o
that the historian is free to express any whim or ca|

hard relativist maintains that the ideal of a value-free history is impossible, and this implies both that history cannot be objective and that historical knowledge is impossible. As we will see shortly, serious difficulties afflict both hard objectivism and hard relativism.

Soft relativism and soft objectivism deemphasize the second (valuational) sense of historical objectivity in favor of the first (history as subject to critical revision). According to *soft relativism,* even though historical writing may evidence the presence of the historian's subjectivity, history can still avoid being arbitrary by remaining open to evaluation by objective canons of evidence and truth. The work of every historian will reflect more or less the interests, values, and world view of the writer. Some perspectivism and distortion may be unavoidable. Nonetheless, what the historian produces from his perspective is open to criticism and revision. Thus while any historical account will be relative to some degree, it is capable of being objective in the sense that it is correctable; it is subject to revision and thus is not arbitrary.

As I use the term, *soft objectivism* does not differ from soft relativism in any significant way. The major difference between the two is the direction from which one arrives at the position. The mediating position may be approached by correcting the excesses of hard objectivism; in this case, the person holding the mediating view could be regarded as a soft objectivist. Or the more moderate view could be approached as a reaction to the excesses of hard relativism, in which case the person could be called a soft relativist.

My point can be clarified by means of two schema. The first builds on my earlier distinction between four possible positions on the subject of historical objectivity:

HARD RELATIVISM	SOFT RELATIVISM
History is both subjective (value-laden) and arbitrary.	History is subjective but need not be arbitrary.

HARD OBJECTIVISM	SOFT OBJECTIVISM
History can rise above the historian's subjectivity and be value-free.	History can never be completely free from the values of the historian; but this does not mean that history is arbitrary since it is open to critical revision.

I then pointed out that if these four options are placed on a continuum, hard relativism and hard objectivism represent the most extreme positions while soft relativism and soft objectivism tend to blur into each other so that we effectively end up with three basic positions as follows:

HARD RELATIVISM	SOFT RELATIVISM	HARD OBJECTIVISM
	or SOFT OBJECTIVISM	

In considering the viability of these three options, it hardly seems necessary to waste any time critiquing hard objectivism. Why beat a horse that has been dead for several generations? Whatever the value of their own theories may have been, idealists like Dilthey, Croce, and Collingwood unveiled the folly of any quest for history as it really was. The nineteenth-century model of a scientific history was an oversimplified distortion of the historian's enterprise. However, hard relativism is still regarded as a viable option in some circles. A careful evaluation of the position and the arguments offered in its support seems necessary.

An Evaluation of Hard Relativism

One of the better-known cases for hard relativism is found in Charles A. Beard's essay "That Noble

Dream.''* According to Beard, ''the historian's powers are limited. He may search for, but he cannot find
the 'objective truth' of history or write it 'as it actually
was.' ''[95] Beard's case in support of historical relativism can be reduced to four major arguments. For
one thing, the historian can never know his subject
matter *directly*. All knowledge of the past is *indirect*
and *inferential*. Thus the historian cannot begin with
the past; he must start with that which is present to
him (his sources) and work his way back into the past.
Second, Beard argued that the historian's knowledge
of his subject matter is necessarily *incomplete*. The
historian is forced by the sheer mass of evidence to
select his facts. But this presupposes a criterion of
selection that varies from one historian to another.
Third, Beard pointed out that historians do not simply
accept *passively* what their sources tell them. They
must approach their sources critically, much the way
a lawyer cross-examines his witnesses. If historical
inquiry is to be productive, it must have a direction
from its inception. But as Beard saw it, any admission
that historical inquiry is goal-directed implies that it is
prejudiced from the start. Finally, the hard relativists
insist, historical investigation is value-charged. History is not discovered so much as it is constructed, a
process inseparable from the historian's own subjective concerns, interests, and prejudices.

For several decades, many historians accepted
Beard's conclusions at face value. More recently,
however, Beard's arguments have been subjected to
analysis that reveals that his attempt to resolve the
problem of historical objectivity in favor of hard relativism was a false start. Most of his arguments turn
out to be inconclusive, and the one track he tried that
has merit was stated far too vaguely to be much good.
We will now examine Beard's four major arguments.

---

*Charles A. Beard (1876–1948) was a distinguished American
historian, perhaps best known for his controversial but influential
book *An Economic Interpretation of the Constitution* (New York:
Macmillan, 1913). His essay on which my remarks are based was
originally delivered as a presidential address to the American Historical Association. It has been reprinted many times. See Ronald
Nash, *Ideas of History*, 2:162–76.

I will first restate them and then note the more serious objections.

1. Several of Beard's arguments for historical relativism appeal to the undisputed claim that *the historian's knowledge of the past is indirect*. While the claim is true, Beard overstated the entailments of his claim. Beard phrased his point in this way:

> The historian is not an observer of the past that lies beyond his own time. He cannot see it *objectively* as the chemist sees his test tubes and compounds. The historian must "see" the actuality of history through the medium of documentation. That is his sole recourse.[96]

When Beard asserts that what the historian seeks to know (the past) no longer exists and that the historian's access to the past must be mediated by documents and records that exist in his present, he is correct. More problematic is Beard's attempt to set up a contrast between scientific knowledge (like chemistry), where the subject matter is supposedly observable in a direct manner and thus objective, and history, where the approach is indirect and thus relative. In other words, his first argument for relativism seems to equate relativism with indirect knowledge and objectivism with direct knowledge. His position rests on the claim that A can know B if and only if A can directly inspect B. Unfortunately, Beard's claim implies that a person cannot have knowledge of anything that cannot be inspected directly. What Beard forgot is that a great deal of scientific investigation, which he regards as a paradigm of objectivity, also proceeds in an indirect manner. When an astronomer peers through a telescope, he does not perceive the object of his vision directly. Light from the star or planet he is studying has been reflected many times before it reaches his eyes; this makes his knowledge indirect. A similar problem affects scientific knowledge that is mediated by instruments like microscopes, cloud chambers, and the like. Beard's first line of argument, then, would not only destroy the historian's knowledge of the past, it would also nullify any scientific claim to knowledge that is indirect. Furthermore, Beard's argument would exclude scientific claims to knowledge based on past experiments. Suppose a scientist begins working on a particular problem where earlier scientists conducting previous experiments have established a set of conclusions from which further work can begin. Imagine further that this scientist himself has not performed all of those earlier experiments. Any conclusion derived from the prior work of others and not verified personally by our scientist would be *indirect* knowledge. Beard apparently would say that such conclusions do not qualify as knowledge, and on this position every scientist would have to repeat every experiment relevant to his current investigation. Finally, Beard's argument would rule out indirect knowledge about things or events occurring at other places. We conclude then that if there is a good case for hard relativism, it cannot be based on the claim that the historian's knowledge of his subject matter is indirect.

2. Beard based his second line of argument for historical relativism on the claim that *the historian's knowledge of the past is incomplete*. The historian can seldom be sure he has assembled all of the possible and relevant documentation. Once again Beard begins with an indisputable observation but draws an invalid inference. Just because a historian cannot know *everything* about the past, does it follow that he cannot know *anything* about it? Does it follow that his knowledge is tainted by relativity? Of course it doesn't. The box score of a baseball game is not complete; it does not report everything about the ball game. But the incompleteness of the account of the box score doesn't necessitate that it is false. Incomplete knowledge is not necessarily false. Incomplete human knowledge may still be true as far as it goes. Therefore Beard's second argument involves a serious confusion between the incompleteness of an account and its falsity. But Beard's argument also ignores the fact that no human inquiry presents a full report about its subject. Physics and biology, no less than history, give incomplete reports. But as we have seen, Beard has no desire to impugn the objectivity of the natural sciences. However, contrary to Beard, if the incomplete accounts found in the natural sciences can be

objective, then so too can the incomplete accounts of the historian be objective. Nor does much of significance follow from the fact that historical inquiry is selective. While it is true that no historian can include everything he knows in his narrative, it is also true that *all human inquiry is selective to some degree;* no academic inquiry simply reproduces its subject matter. As American theologian Van Harvey notes, "If selectivity is the precondition for knowing or relating anything at all, how can its existence be used as an argument for the impossibility of any objective historical knowledge?"[97] The mere presence of selectivity in an account does not by itself compromise the objective truth of that account, since some selections can be more plausible, have more support, and be more reasonable than others. It is also important to notice how many times historians select material that leads to truth that runs counter to what their own values would have led them to hope to find. Harvey observes that this kind of hard relativism under scrutiny

> assumes that selection always involves distortion, that interest and purpose are necessarily antithetical to objectivity. But these assumptions acquire their force only by holding an impossible and irrelevant ideal up before the historian, namely that he should reproduce the past in the way some divine observer with no interests and purposes would. But this comparison, surely, only breeds confusion. The question whether history can be objective or not is a genuine one only if real alternatives exist. The issue is not whether historians are to be compared with an omniscient divine observer, but whether *within* the limits of human observation, which is necessarily selective, there are some standards for judging the degree of arbitrariness of selection and for adjudicating historical disputes. The question of objectivity is not, "Can a historian see as God sees?" It is, "Are there canons which enable the human historian to judge whether some things are true, even if they run counter to what he devoutly hopes and wishes were not true?[98]

3. Beard grounded his third argument on the fact that *the historian must impose some kind of structure or form on history.* Without an overarching pattern, the historian would have only a mass of unrelated

data. This structure is *not discovered* in the past; it is *imposed on* the past by the historian. But as noted earlier, Beard once again oversimplifies the situation and ignores the extent to which any science is forced to provide a structure for its material. The problem of structuring a subject matter is not unique to history and thus does not ground the claim that history is relative or subjective. What destroys objectivity is not the arrangement of data but the ignoring or twisting of data.

4. While Beard's first three lines of attack against the possibility of objective knowledge in history are less than impressive, his fourth basic argument is much more serious and will require more attention. Beard argues that *the historian's account of the past is unavoidably value-charged.* By this Beard meant that the historian's selection of material and the structure he imposes on that material will necessarily be affected by his own world view, interests, biases, etc.

Those who believe that the unavoidable presence of value judgments in the historian's work necessarily implies hard relativism ignore the important difference between psychology and logic. It is one thing to study the *psychological process* by which a historian formulates his beliefs and another thing to study the *logical process* by which those beliefs can be justified. In his actual work, the historian may be influenced by a number of cultural and psychological factors as well as personal quirks and prejudices. But however his conclusions are reached, that work can always be evaluated by criteria that make the presence of the valuational element much less significant than hard relativists have thought. It is important not to confuse the processes of discovery and justification. The process of discovering the past may be influenced by any number of psychological and social factors. But when the historian turns to the matter of justifying his interpretations, his psychological quirks and prejudices, his background, and his interests should become irrelevant.[99] Implicit in the analysis of Beard's fourth argument is my earlier distinction between two senses of historical objectivity. I am admitting that the actual work of the historian in selecting and organizing his data and then describing the past may be inescapably tied to that historian's own values. But that historian's work can always be challenged; and when it is, his evidence, reasoning, and interpretations will be subject to critical revision.

**Objections to
Hard Relativism**

Not only is hard relativism difficult to support, it is also a position vulnerable to several serious objections. For one thing, hard relativism entails the belief that there *is no difference between good history and bad history,* an absurd conclusion to be sure. If hard relativism were true, any distinction between truth and error in history would disappear, historical knowledge would become impossible, and it is difficult to see how history could merit any respect as a cognitive discipline. As long as there is a difference between history and propaganda and between good history and bad history, some historical writing must be capable in principle of rising above the personal biases of the historian. While some perspectivism and distortion may be unavoidable, what the historian produces from his perspective is open to criticism and revision.

Second, hard relativism entails *historical skepticism.* Since the various points of view taken by historians are, according to the relativist, subjective, there is no possible way to settle disputes among historians. Between different historians and the past, there is an insurmountable wall that makes any knowledge of the past impossible.

Third, hard relativism is *inconsistent with assumptions that are inseparable from any scholarly enterprise.* Norman Geisler writes:

> Why strive for accuracy unless it is believed that the revision is more objectively true than the previous view? Why critically analyze unless improvement toward a more accurate view is the assumed goal? Perfect objectivity may be practically unattainable within the limited resources of the historian on most if not all topics. But be this as it may, the inability to attain 100 percent objectivity is a long way from total relativity. Reaching a degree

of objectivity which is subject to criticism and revision is a more realistic conclusion than the relativist's arguments. In short, there is no reason to eliminate the possibility of a sufficient degree of historical objectivity.[100]

The fact that historians continually rewrite their accounts of the past in an effort to achieve greater accuracy shows how inapplicable is Beard's understanding of history to the actual work of historians.

Fourth, it is important to note that hard relativism in history or in any other discipline is self-defeating. Once again Norman Geisler puts this well:

> For either their [the hard relativists'] view is historically conditioned and, therefore, unobjective or else it is not relative but objective. If the latter, then it thereby admits that it is possible to be objective in viewing history. On the contrary, if the position of historical relativism is itself relative, then it cannot be taken as objectively true. It is simply subjective opinion which has no basis to claim to be objectively true about all of history. In short, if it is a subjective opinion it cannot eliminate the possibility that history is objectively knowable; and if it is an objective fact about history then objective facts can be known about history. In the first case objectivity is not eliminated and in the second relativity is self-defeated. Hence, in either case, objectivity is possible.[101]

I hasten to add that the objectivity that is possible is what I earlier called soft objectivity.

Conclusion

Christianity has an obvious stake in the debate over historical objectivity. If hard relativism were plausible, a serious challenge to the historical integrity of the New Testament documents could be mounted on the grounds that those documents are colored by the partisan interests of committed believers. But as we have seen, historical objectivism has not been regarded as a live option for generations. If hard relativism were true, Christianity would be open to attack from a different direction. Since Christianity is a religion uniquely dependent on the historicity of certain past events, the total skepticism about the past that is entailed by hard relativism would undermine the historical ground of the Christian faith and radically alter the *nature* of the faith. But we have noted that the hard relativist's arguments against the possibility of objective historical knowledge are tainted and his own position is subject to a number of devastating objections.

By all accounts, then, both Christian and secular historians are stuck with options somewhere between hard objectivism and hard relativism. Even though *complete* objectivity may be an impossible dream, historical investigation can in principle be freed from the historian's subjective interests and biases. To the extent that historical objectivity is understood in the sense of being open to critical investigation and re-examination, it seems that historical objectivity is possible. Yale professor Nils Alstrup Dahl relates these conclusions to historical research about Jesus:

> The fact that objectively assured results can only be reached in an approximate way does not in itself distinguish Jesus-research from other historical science. The point is rather that the difficulties with which *all* historical science must grapple are especially perceptible in this area. All historical work is influenced by the presuppositions of the historian, and he himself is a child of his own time. That becomes particularly noticeable when Jesus is made the object of historical research, and even the historian obviously cannot deal with Jesus without being involved in a positive or negative way. It is a real question whether personal involvement is not a positive presupposition for a scholar's attaining to any kind of historically fruitful results. To a certain degree, wishful thinking and subjective errors can be eliminated by methodically scientific work, when the will to truth is present. Scholars with different starting points co-operate and are able mutually to correct each other.[102]

Dahl has a point. Is a historian with a strongly negative bias toward the person and teaching of Jesus as described in the New Testament really in a stronger position to discover the truth than someone who approaches his subject matter with a degree of interest and sympathy? Bias can be a two-edged sword in the sense that it can both inspire people to see things that aren't there and lead others to ignore things that are there.

There is a myth abroad in the land that holds that a

historical approach that a priori rules out the possibility of the miraculous is more scientific and more open-minded than a supernaturalistic view that allows for the truth of biblical accounts of miracles. This so-called scientific history is actually under the control of a *naturalistic world view*. Basic to the naturalistic world view is the conviction that the world is a closed system, that is, the world is not open to any causal factors beyond the natural laws of the material universe. Anything that happens within the natural universe must be explained in terms of other natural causes. When applied to history, this naturalism "assumes an unbroken chain of cause and effects in the flow of history. . . . the 'scientific' method excludes the possibility of the supernatural before it has studied the evidence. It is based on a philosophical presupposition about the nature of historical reality."[103] George Ladd goes on to point out the irony of this: "This utterly anti-miraculous, naturalistic approach to the biblical history is supposed to be more 'scientific' and 'objective' than a method that recognizes the reality of the supernatural."[104] Ladd objects to this simplistic and close-minded view on the grounds that "a truly scientific method is the inductive method which accepts as a working hypothesis the *best explanation for the known facts.*"[105] Applying his claim to the resurrection of Jesus, Ladd continues:

> There are certain known "historical" facts which we will shortly discuss; the death and burial of Jesus; the discouragement and disillusionment of the disciples; their sudden transformation to be witnesses to Jesus' resurrection; the empty tomb; the rise of the Christian church; and the conversion of Saul. The "historical method" must come up with a satisfying, convincing "historical" explanation for this set of facts. It is our contention that no such historical explanation has yet been produced and that the best hypothesis to account for the known "facts," indeed, the only adequate hypothesis, is that God raised Jesus from the dead in bodily form. However, the so-called "scientific" method excludes the possibility of this hypothesis at the very outset. Far from being open-minded and "objective," it is close-minded to one of the most viable explanations. If there is a living God who is

the Lord of history, who has chosen to act in historical events as the Bible witnesses, the "scientific method" has no way of recognising that fact. On the contrary, the very presuppositions of the scientific method make it blind to one very live option. In other words, the scepticism of such scholars as Bultmann and Marxsen is not due to problems which arise as a result of an inductive study of the texts: it is due rather to the presupposition that a literal bodily resurrection to which our Gospels witness is excluded. The man of faith is therefore more open-minded than the so-called scientific historian.[106]

As we have seen, the kind of closed-minded attitude that, under the control of naturalistic presuppositions, decides before the fact to reject certain evidence is not reserved exclusively for certain secular historians. It is also an inherent part of the historical approach of some Christian theologians, Rudolf Bultmann and his followers being notable examples.

Everyone who attempts to learn the historical truth about the life and teaching of Jesus, about his death and resurrection, and about how convictions about that death and resurrection gave birth to the Christian church will be biased to some extent. Are some biases better or worse than others? In this particular subject area, perhaps some are. Certainly a bias that unconsciously leads a historian to say that regardless of the evidence, he knows *before the fact* that certain kinds of things could not have happened is not a bias conducive to an open-minded historical investigation. Unbelieving historians need to give greater attention to their commitment to a naturalistic world view; they need to reexamine the extent to which their naturalistic presuppositions control the way they handle their data. Perhaps the historian whose world view is open to the possibility of the miraculous holds a position that is more deserving of the label of "scientific."

chapter six

Historical Facts and Their Meaning

The relationship between facts and their meaning is examined, with special emphasis on what is meant by objectivity. Pannenberg's contention that fact and interpretation cannot be separated is also considered.

Considerable confusion surrounds what are called the "facts" of history. Some people write as if historical investigation is grounded on a solid bedrock composed of such facts. Others question what a fact of history is and raise the possibility that even if such facts exist in some sense, they are not the starting point for historical investigation but only an end result of reflection about history.

The preceding chapter drew attention to two extreme positions advanced with regard to historical objectivity. There is a similar continuum with respect to historical facts. On the one hand, there are those who write as if history is laden with *brute facts* just waiting to be discovered; this view has obvious   93 affinities to the position of the hard objectivist. If such brute facts did exist, all that the historian would have to do to provide an objective account of the past is *discover* the facts and report them truthfully. Once the brute facts of history have been uncovered, those who hold this view maintain, it will be immediately clear to any unbiased observer what the facts mean. Such a view of history minimizes (and in its most extreme form eliminates) the subjectivity of the historian.

At the other extreme can be found the position of historians like Carl Becker who challenge the infatuation with brute facts.[107] As Becker sees it, the so-called facts of history are not discovered so much as they are created; they don't exist "out there" (whatever this phrase might mean), but they exist rather in the present consciousness of historians. Becker's analysis of historical facts has obvious affinities to C. A. Beard's hard relativism.

The debate over the nature and existence of historical facts is relevant to Christian theology in several ways. For one thing, one's position on this question will affect one's view of historical objectivity (and vice versa), and we have already seen the stake that the Christian student of history has in the problem of objectivity. Moreover, reflective Christians will want to make a decision regarding the merit of attempts to defend Christianity exclusively through appeals to historical facts. In addition, our study of historical facts will introduce us to the vital matter of the relationship between so-called facts and their interpretation or meaning. Perhaps the key question in history is the *hermeneutical* one: How do we come to understand the past? T. A. Roberts has expressed it in this way:

> To state what is a historical "fact" presupposes some principle of interpretation, which determines the historian's assessment of what is "fact" and what is not. In short, one cannot inquire into the history of the past without bringing to the task a prior principle of interpretation. The answers to historical questions will be partly determined by the presuppositions which bias the framing of the questions themselves.[108]

Carl Becker* began his famous discussion of the problem by asking, What is a "fact" of history? He asked his readers to contemplate the "fact" that Julius Caesar crossed the Rubicon in 49 B.C. Without doubt, Caesar did cross that particular river in that particular year. But so did his entire army, including many soldiers, horses, and supplies. In other words, Caesar's crossing was accompanied by thousands of acts, words, and thoughts. It is no exaggeration to say, then, as Becker did, that "a thousand and one lesser 'facts' went to make up the one simple fact that Caesar crossed the Rubicon. . . . Thus the simple fact turns out to be not a simple fact at all. It is the statement [that Caesar crossed the Rubicon] that is simple."[109] Becker was not denying that the original event actually occurred. But he was pointing out that many so-called facts of history are a shorthand way of referring to a much larger complex of events. But this means that there is a sense in which many so-called facts of history are a construct, a fiction, a symbol, and an interpretation that results from the historian's interaction with historical sources.

First, the fact is a construct, because it is not something the historian "discovers" per se. It is a conclusion the historian reaches after deciding to omit a great deal from the original event, after deciding to telescope a much larger complex of events into a simpler shorthand statement. Second, many facts are a fiction in the sense that taken literally, there is a discrepancy between the simple truth they report and the much more complex set of truths they summarize. Taken literally and by itself, "Caesar crossed the Rubicon" suggests that just one man forded that river on that day. But as we have seen, "Caesar" stands for the general and his entire army and everything else that accompanied his military force on its historic march to Rome. Third, the fact is also a symbol. In most cases, it would be inconvenient or even impossible to continue referring to every detail of the

Carl Becker's Analysis of Historical Fact

---

*Carl Becker (1873–1945) was an eminent American historian whose books included *The Declaration of Independence* (1922) and *The Heavenly City of the Eighteenth-Century Philosophers* (1932).

original event. Thus, it is useful to have an expression that refers to the much more complex original event. The fact in question, then, is not that larger event but the simple sentence "Caesar crossed the Rubicon" that serves as a symbol for the larger event.* Finally, the fact is itself the product of the historian's personal interaction with his sources. During the course of history, many people besides Caesar crossed the Rubicon. But no one ever talks about the time, for example, when Publius crossed the Rubicon as a fact of history. Why not? It is because Caesar's crossing is judged important since it is tied to a complex of other events that have significance in the course of later history.

> Apart from these great events and complicated rela-
> tions, the crossing of the Rubicon means nothing, it is not
> a historical fact properly speaking at all. In itself it is
> nothing for us; it becomes something for us, not in itself,
> but as a symbol of something else, a symbol standing for
> a long series of events which have to do with the most
> intangible realities, *viz.*, the relation between Caesar and
> the millions of people of the Roman world.[110]

Whatever objections we may yet raise to Becker's theory, he is correct in drawing attention to the simplistic way in which some writers about history refer to historical facts. The facts of history are quite different from specific things like bricks or rocks, just waiting "out there" for some historian to trip over, notice, pick up, and interpret. A fact of history is something far more elusive and intangible than this. Becker's idealistic analysis of facts was not a denial of the original events for which the facts stood. But those events no longer exist; therefore the historian cannot investigate those events directly. What the historian deals with directly are statements that the particular event took place. According to Becker:

---

*In Becker's words: "Thus the simple historical fact turns out to be not a hard, cold something with clear outline, and measurable pressure, like a brick. It is so far as we know it, only a *symbol,* a statement which is a generalization of a thousand and one simpler facts which we do not for the moment care to use, and this generalization itself we cannot use apart from the wider facts and generalizations which it symbolizes" (p. 180).

When we really get down to the hard facts, what the historian is always dealing with is an *affirmation*—an affirmation of the fact that something is true. There is thus a distinction of capital importance to be made: the distinction between the ephemeral event which disappears, and the affirmation about the event that constitutes for us the historical fact. If so the historical fact is not the past event, but a symbol which enables us to re-create it imaginatively.[111]

Becker's understanding of the nature of historical fact demands that historical facts don't exist "out there" but rather in the mind of the historian. At some point in the past the original occurrence existed out there, independently of people's minds. But of course the original occurrence is gone; it has vanished. Caesar's act of crossing the Rubicon no longer exists per se.

How can the historian deal with vanished realities? He can deal with them because these vanished realities give place to pale reflections, impalpable images or ideas of themselves, and these pale reflections, and impalpable images which cannot be touched or handled are all that is left of the actual occurrences. These are therefore what the historian deals with. These are his "material." He has to be satisfied with these, for the very good reason that he has nothing else. . . . Where are the facts? They are, as I said before, in his mind, or in somebody's mind, or they are nowhere.[112]

It will not do to counter that the facts are in historical records or sources. Obviously this claim is true.

At all events, the historical facts lying dead in the records can do nothing good or evil in the world. They become historical facts, capable of doing work, of making a difference, only when someone, you or I, brings them alive in our minds by means of pictures, images, or ideas of the actual occurrence. For this reason I say that the historical fact is in someone's mind, or it is nowhere, because when it is in no one's mind it lies in the records inert, incapable of making a difference in the world.[113]

As Becker used the term, facts are *not given* to the historian; facts are *not discovered*. Instead, the historian *creates facts* as his interests interact with his sources. Facts are not the starting point for the historian. Rather, they are already one *end result* of his work.

Becker's theory certainly calls for analysis and evaluation. On the one hand, his view is an important and necessary corrective to the simple-minded belief that the historian looks for brute facts while sifting through what has survived from the past. Becker is right in pointing out how the historian's subjectivity is inseparable from every stage of his work, even the determination of what shall count as a "fact." But if Becker's theory is pushed too far, it can be taken to mean that there is never any "hard" evidence to correct or falsify a particular historical claim. Such a view of course would in practical terms be indistinguishable from the position of hard relativism and would be open to all of the difficulties that afflict that theory.

How much of the dispute over historical facts is a verbal dispute? That is, to what extent is the disagreement more apparent than real because the key word *fact* is used in different senses? In an important sense, Becker's distinction between a fact (a symbolic, shorthand affirmation) and the event to which the fact refers is correct. But people often use the word *fact* to refer not to such statements about the event but to the event itself. The word is also used to refer to something that people know with certainty. In this usage, "it is certain" and "it is a fact" are used synonymously. Sometimes the word is used with reference to something that really exists, as opposed to being imaginary or illusory. And finally, people often use "fact" in regard to something that they believe has been objectively verified; in this usage, something not a fact would still lack sufficient verification.

Thus, it appears, Becker has provided a helpful analysis of *one* meaning of the word *fact*. But the usage to which he refers may not be the most common, and people who appeal to facts of history in ways that differ from his analysis may not be guilty of the brute-fact fallacy. Christian theologians and apologists who talk about *the fact of Christ's resurrection* may be using the phrase in any of the following ways:

1. as a short-hand reference for the entire complex of events surrounding the resurrection (Becker's sense).
2. as a way of expressing their confidence that the resurrection really happened, that is, as a synonymous way of saying that the resurrection is certain.
3. as a way of claiming that the resurrection really happened in the objective world of space and time. That is, the disciples did not simply imagine the resurrection.
4. as an expression of the belief that there is sufficient evidence to verify the historicity of the resurrection.

Therefore, Becker's analysis of "fact" is helpful as far as it goes, provided that one does not push it too far. He is right in pointing out, contrary to the *brute-fact theorists,* that historical facts as presented in narratives are always human constructions; but this observation implies nothing about the truth of any historical claim or the sufficiency of evidence for it.

Facts and Their Interpretation

One of the more important things that does follow from Becker's analysis is that there is no such thing as a narrative-fact apart from some interpretation. In this regard, a view like Becker's in which facts are inseparable from their interpretation follows the trend of contemporary historiography. The positivist search for bare facts apart from any interpretation has been discredited. For reasons to be noted shortly, the Christian theologian and historian welcomes the contemporary conjoining of facts and faith, of history and interpretation. The work of the German theologian Wolfhart Pannenberg illustrates one way in which this closer alignment of fact and meaning can service important Christian convictions.*

---

*Pannenberg, who was born in 1928, is one of the more influential theologians on the contemporary scene. He is a professor of theology at the University of Munich. In spite of Pannenberg's prominence in contemporary discussions about the relationship between the Christian faith and history, it is difficult to find a systematic and complete discussion of his position in any of his

Pannenberg argues that it is wrong to separate fact and interpretation (meaning). Brute facts do not exist; facts always come within some context of meaning. But Pannenberg does not think that one must have faith *before* he can discover God's revelation in the history of the Old or New Testaments. Instead, Pannenberg holds, all we must do is approach the events with an open mind. An impartial observation of the events will generate true faith.

The first question that arises from Pannenberg's claims concerns his suggestion that if the facts of history are approached with an open, unbiased mind, they will yield only one conclusion, that is, the correct conclusion. At first glance, Pannenberg's claim appears false. Is it not true that the same facts can not only give rise to diverse interpretations but also lead to false ones? Many times, it seems, there is no logically sufficient connection between some fact and its correct interpretation. Consider an example from the account of the virgin birth of Christ in the Gospel of Matthew. Let us imagine, if we can, what might have happened if both Mary and Joseph had been left uninformed about the meaning of her pregnancy. Had the angels not conveyed an interpretation of Mary's pregnancy to Mary and Joseph, there would have been two extremely puzzled people in Nazareth. By all appearances, the mere fact of Mary's pregnancy did not carry its own interpretation. Note further that angelic visitation was necessary to give Mary and Joseph the *correct* interpretation. Matthew 1:19ff. shows that Joseph had interpreted the facts but had come to the *wrong* conclusion. Does Pannenberg's theory not clash with the indisputable evidence that historical facts often give rise to diverse and even incorrect interpretations? I think not.

The objection in view ignores a crucial qualification that Pannenberg adds. Pannenberg believes historical facts are logically sufficient to imply the correct interpretation when viewed *within their proper*

---

works to this date. My discussion draws from several sources, including his *Revelation as History* (New York: Macmillan, 1968) and *Faith and Reality* (Philadelphia: Westminster, 1977).

context. Consider the case of a father who takes his son to his first baseball game in Atlanta, Georgia. Both are eyewitnesses to the same events. They both see the little white ball hit over the fence and hear the crowd yell with excitement. They both hear people talking about home run number 715. The number *715* keeps flashing on scoreboards all over the park. The father is ecstatic, but all the little boy can ask is, "What happened?" Is this not a case where two people are unbiased eyewitnesses to the same facts in a situation in which those facts fail, in one case, to produce the *right* interpretation? Pannenberg can answer this question in the negative by pointing out that the two eyewitnesses (father and son) are not really dealing with the same and complete set of facts. The meaning of Hank Aaron's 715th home run is not confined to the home run itself. After all, he had performed similar feats on at least 714 previous occasions. Being an eyewitness to the event in question includes an understanding of *the entire context* in which the event took place: the rules of baseball, its history, its schedule, it records, and so on. Once this context is seen as an inseparable part of the event known as *Hank Aaron's 715th home run,* the meaning and significance of the event does follow.

When the apostle Paul maintains that Christian faith is grounded on the fact of Christ's resurrection, he means that it is based both on what happened (Christ arose) and what it means. The Bible not only reports the resurrection, it also interprets it, and that interpretation takes into account the context in which the resurrection took place. That context includes a divinely revealed interpretation of the event such as those given by Paul in Romans 1:4 and 1 Corinthians 15. Alan Richardson explains this well:

> It is not, then, the historical events as such which are themselves the content of the special revelation through history, since without the prophetic interpretation of events no revelation would be given through them. It must be in some way the whole complex of the events together with their interpretation which constitutes the revelation of God in history.[114]

This means that the *meaning* of the event has its ground in history. It would be a mistake to think that the fact occurs in history and the interpretation comes from somewhere else. The angelic interpretation of Mary's pregnancy was part of the whole context of the event. When the "fact" of Hank Aaron's 715th home run is seen to include as its context the history and records of baseball, what happened that night in Atlanta's Fulton County Stadium does provide, for anyone who knows that full context, sufficient grounds for determining the meaning of what happened. When the fact of Christ's resurrection includes everything relevant to its context, that fact provides sufficient grounds, for anyone aware of the total context, for determining the meaning of the empty tomb.

We have been considering the relationship between facts and their meaning. Whereas positivist historians divorce fact and interpretation, the trend both in secular philosophy of history and in Christian theology of history is to view fact and meaning as conjoined. The relationship between facts and interpretation is explained either in a subjective or an objective way. According to philosopher Maurice Mandelbaum, the subjective view holds that the interpretation of events proceeds from the subject whereas the objective approach claims that an interpretation is "forced upon the subject by the nature of the material with which he is dealing."[115] These two possibilities can be pictured as follows:

A	*B*
SUBJECT (interests/values of historian)	OBJECT (event or fact)
↓	↓
OBJECT (event or fact)	INTERPRETATION (forced by material)
↓	↓
INTERPRETATION (proceeds from subject)	SUBJECT (interests/values play no part)

In *B,* the nature of the object (the event or fact) is such that it naturally forces a particular interpretation upon the subject. In *A,* the dominance of the features within the subject (interests, world view, values, etc.) is such that they affect the way the subject apprehends the object and thus *determines* the interpretation. But a third alternative is also possible:

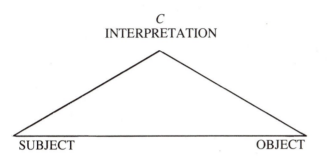

C
INTERPRETATION

SUBJECT   OBJECT

According to option *C,* an interpretation of historical data has two horizons. Any correct interpretation must be consistent with the full context of the event or fact, as explained earlier. But no interpretation can proceed in isolation from the subjectivity of the interpreter. If the interpreter had no initial interest in the topic, it is unlikely that he would even begin his study. If he did not regard a piece of evidence as relevant or important, that record or artifact would never be included among his "facts." The historian is in no danger of being replaced by a computer. A personal and human element is an unavoidable part of writing history. It is a mistake, however, to exaggerate the place of the subject to the point that the objective evidence no longer serves as a guide to what he writes or as a check to his enthusiasm. The subjective approach to the relation of fact and meaning (theory *A*) would leave us sinking in a morass of relativity. If our only option were the choice between the subjective theory *(A)* and the objective theory *(B),* the latter is clearly more acceptable. All truth including historical truth is transpersonal. The difficulty of the objective theory *(B)* lies not in what it says but in what it fails to say. The meaning and interpretation of historical events and facts must flow from those objective events and facts, to be sure. But there could be no interpretation without an interested, value-directed subject to begin the investigation, to sift through the evidence, to organize the data, etc.

To summarize, I would agree with Pannenberg that the subjectivist model of interpretation *(A)* must be rejected. I also agree that the positivist or Neo-Kantian approach that separates fact and meaning must also be avoided. Theologian James Robinson is right when he states:

> Such a splitting up of historical consciousness into a detection of facts and an evaluation of them (or into history as known and history as experienced) is intolerable to Christian faith, not only because the message of the resurrection of Jesus and of God's revelation in him necessarily becomes merely subjective interpretation, but also because it is the reflection of an outmoded and questionable historical method. It is based on the futile aim of the positivist historians to ascertain bare facts without meaning in history.[116]

Against the positivist separation of fact and meaning, Robinson explains:

> We must reinstate today the original unity of facts and their meaning. Every event, if not artificially taken out of context (out of its historical environment, stretching into the past and the future), brings its own meaning for each particular inquirer, brings it with its context, which of course is always a context of tradition. Admittedly not every event has equal clarity of meaning. This differs from case to case. But, in principle, every event has its original meaning within the context of occurrence and tradition in which it took place and through which it is connected with the present and its historical interest. In spite of our statement that the meaning of an event is inherent to its original context and is not something injected into it by the interpreter, nevertheless that meaning can be determined only in relation to the vantage point of the particular inquirer. The reason for this is that the historical continuum within which an event has meaning also includes the present. But one may not arbitrarily attach whatever meaning one will to a given fact. Only

when the original unity of event and meaning is grasped may the question of the historicity of Jesus' resurrection be properly raised again.[117]

In the above paragraph Robinson summarizes several points that were made in my own presentation: (1) Fact and meaning must not be separated. (2) Fact carries with it a context that varies obviously with the event. (3) This context stretches back into the past before the event and continues into the future after the event. (4) If the event is to be understood, it must not be artificially divorced from its context. (5) When viewed properly, which means examined without prejudice and studied within its context, the meaning of the event will emerge. (6) The meaning of the event is inseparable from its original context. The correct meaning of an event is never something that the interpreter forces on the event. Thus the content of the event (along with its context) constitutes one horizon of the interpretation of the fact. (7) But the meaning of an event cannot be completely divorced from the subjectivity of the investigator. As Robinson put it, "The historical continuum within which an event has meaning also includes the present." But this does not permit the interpreter any arbitrariness in the meaning he gives to his fact.

Although my triadic model of interpretation differs from Pannenberg's more objectivist model *(B),* it is still consistent with perhaps the most important insight of Pannenberg's position. As William Hamilton describes it, Pannenberg's view requires that "certainty about the resurrection does not come from the decision of faith. Faith is based on the certainty, which must come from outside of faith."[118] *The objective content of the event or the fact functions as a check against arbitrariness or bias.* Even if one historian succumbs to his own subjectivity and distorts the past, the available evidence can in principle enable other historians to point out his errors.

History and Propositional Revelation

The inseparableness of fact and meaning, of event and interpretation, supports an important tenet of evangelical theology, namely, the insistence that the modes of divine revelation include a communication of truth in inspired propositions. The neoorthodox repudiation of all cognitive revelation in favor of a subjective, noncognitive personal disclosure is theologically and epistemologically unsound.* Traditionally minded Protestants and Catholics recognize that God has not only revealed Himself in certain historical events but that He has also given human beings a propositional revelation that includes the divine interpretation of those events. British theologian Alan Richardson explains, "Revelation is thus due to the twofold form of the activity of God: God controls the historical events which constitute the *media* of revelation, and He also inspires the minds of the prophets and thus enables them to interpret the events aright."[119] God reveals Himself in His mighty acts in history. But these acts require a divinely given interpretation.

For example, the Romans crucified thousands of Jews. From the perspective of event, the crucifixion of Jesus was simply one more instance of Roman legal practice, and many eyewitnesses of the death of Jesus interpreted his crucifixion from this perspective. Likewise, many theologians accept the historicity of Jesus' death but fail to see his death as God's atonement for man's sin. Only through the perspective of God's revelation is Jesus' death seen as what it is, the decisive point in the history of redemption. Biblical revelation is a conjunction of event and the interpretation of that event. As American theologian Kenneth Kantzer puts it:

> According to the Bible, the meaning of the mighty acts of God, including that crowning act of all—God incarnate in Jesus Christ, is not a humanly drawn conclusion based on observation of these acts; rather, the meaning of the act is itself also a divine revelation—God's interpretation of His own divine acts. This revelatory word is given by God to man in just as objective a form as are the acts of God in history. These revelations of truth represent God's interpretations. They are God's meaning of events

---

*The arguments against the neoorthodox position are traced in Ronald Nash, *The Word of God and the Mind of Man* (Grand Rapids: Zondervan, 1982).

in history. . . . Biblical revelation is a continuous interdependent unity of act-revelation and truth-revelation.[120]

Swiss theologian Oscar Cullmann agrees about the dual nature of revelation: "Revelation consists in both—in the event as such and in its interpretation. . . . Not only the interpretation but also the event is regarded as revelation."[121] In distinguishing event from interpretation, Cullmann identifies three separate moments:

> . . . first, the naked event to which the prophet must be an eye-witness and which is perceived by non-believers as well, who are unable to see any revelation in it; second, the revelation of a divine plan being disclosed in the event to the prophet, with which he aligns himself in faith; third, the creation of an association with earlier salvation-historical revelations imparted to other prophets in the reinterpretations of these revelations.[122]

But Cullmann's position that revelation occurs both in historical events *and* in their interpretation is ambiguous. It can mean either (1) that revelation is given in the interrelationship of event and interpretation or (2) that revelation is found first in the bare event (apart from any interpretation) and then secondly in the interpretation distinct from the event. Whatever Cullmann may mean, the only one of these two positions that is consistent with the previous argument of this book is the first.

I have been arguing that divine special revelation is not limited to a personal disclosure of God within the subjective experience of believers or to His mighty acts in history. God also gives a special revelation of His mind in divinely revealed propositions that can both ground subjective religious experience and provide a divinely given interpretation of such historical events as the resurrection. God's revelation in such an event as the Exodus is not the bare event alone. It is an event plus divinely revealed interpretation that serves as part of the context of the objective event.

I began this chapter by pointing out that one's position on historical objectivity must parallel one's stand on historical facts. In my earlier discussion of objectivity in history, I opted for the position I called soft objectivism (or soft relativism). My triadic model of historical interpretation is consistent with that earlier stance. Alan Richardson's comments summarize well my position on these two topics:

> We know of what happened only through the written and interpreted (and therefore subjectivized) history of the biblical record. As we have previously seen, not only does the significance of the event for us depend upon our (or the prophets') admittedly subjective interpretation of it, but the very nature of the event, or even whether it occurred at all, is bound up (as far as our knowledge of it is concerned) with our (or the prophets') subjective appreciation of it. We cannot thus divide the content of revelation into history and interpretation, the objective and the subjective; whatever history in the former sense of the word may be, history in the second sense, written history, is never simply "objective". Any account of historical events is conditioned by the principle of interpretation that has been adopted in the presentation of them. If we do not accept the biblical or prophetic principle of interpretation, it is unlikely that we shall accept the biblical record as true or "objective" history. This does not mean that no historical account can be said to be more objectively true than another; it means that we must revise our notion of what objectivity in history-writing is. We must abandon a "correspondence theory" of truth in favour of a "coherence theory" of truth or objectivity.[123]

A correspondence theory of truth holds that a proposition is true when it corresponds to the way things really are. Whatever merit a correspondence theory of truth may have in other areas of knowledge, it does not seem particularly helpful in history for the simple reason that the past to which our historical propositions are supposed to correspond no longer exists. Our approach to the past can never be direct; our theory of historical truth can never be one of correspondence, since there is, strictly speaking, nothing to which it can correspond.

A coherence theory of truth holds that a proposition is true when it coheres with, fits in with, everything else that we know. A police investigator who is forced to solve a crime on the basis of circumstantial evidence must use the coherence standard of truth. So must the historian in his study of history.

chapter seven

History and the Resurrection of Christ

The author presents the answers of four representative theologians (Bultmann, Barth, Pannenberg, and Ladd) to six crucial questions regarding the historicity of the resurrection of Jesus Christ.

History is most relevant to the Christian faith in connection with the resurrection of Jesus Christ. The resurrection is central to the New Testament. The culmination of each Gospel is the resurrection; it was not just something added on at the end of a story about the life of Jesus. Rather, the life of Jesus was presented as a preparation for his death and the resurrection that followed. Peter's sermon on Pentecost, the birthday of the Christian church, emphasized several times that the Jesus who had died on the cross had been raised from the dead by the power of God. Paul repeatedly explained his otherwise unaccountable conversion to Christianity as a result of his encounter with the risen Christ. Paul summarized the gospel in 111 terms of Christ dying for our sins and rising again the third day (1 Cor. 15:3–4). Paul regarded the resurrection as an event in history supported by the strongest possible eyewitness testimony, including his own (1 Cor. 15:5–8). For Paul, the historicity of the resurrection was a *necessary condition* for the truth of Christianity and the validity of Christian belief (1 Cor. 15:12–19).

Alan Richardson comments on the centrality of the resurrection to Christianity:

> The pervading truth which can be learnt from every part of the Gospels, and not merely from their concluding sections, is that the central conviction of the communities in which and for which they were written was faith in Jesus as the Risen Lord; without this faith the Gospels would not have been written. Faith in the resurrection is not one aspect of the New Testament teaching, but the essence of it.[124]

For the first disciples, A. M. Ramsey notes, "the Gospel without the Resurrection was not merely a Gospel without its final chapter: it was not a Gospel at all. . . . Christian theism is Resurrection theism."[125]

This chapter will examine the answers of *four contemporary thinkers to six basic questions* about the resurrection of Christ. This survey then will serve to identify four basic options regarding the historicity of the resurrection and provide an occasion for relating the position of this book to these options. The four thinkers to be studied are Rudolf Bultmann, Karl Barth, Wolfhart Pannenberg, and George Eldon Ladd. The selection of Bultmann, Barth, and Pannenberg requires no special justification. Ladd is included as a representative of contemporary conservative or evangelical theology in America. While not all American conservatives agree with everything Ladd says, he does represent a conservatism that seeks to be faithful to a high view of Scripture while also attempting to hold a responsible position with regard to historical criticism. Ladd's book *I Believe in the Resurrection of Jesus*[126] deals responsibly with the issues as well as with competing views. Further, we might add, many books written on this subject fail—to their detriment—even to deal with the view Ladd represents.

The chapter will examine the answers of these four thinkers to six questions:

1. What is the *essence* or *meaning* of the resurrection for each thinker?

2. Did the resurrection happen in *space* and *time?*

3. Was the resurrection *publicly observable?*

4. Is the resurrection *verifiable* in the same way that other historical events are?

5. Does history provide *total* support, *partial* support, or *no* support for belief in the resurrection?

6. Given what each thinker means by the resurrection, can the resurrection for that thinker be known *apart from history?*

1. The first question, *What is the essence or meaning of the resurrection?* is necessary because different thinkers interpret the resurrection in significantly different ways. Every Easter many believing laypeople hear their pastors deliver eloquent homilies about the resurrection. Unaware of the subtleties of modern theological training, they naturally assume that their pastors are referring to the biblical miracle of God's raising Jesus from the dead. That is, they understand the resurrection claim as referring to something that happened objectively in history. Many theologians and pastors, however, continue to use the word *resurrection* to refer to something quite different. For some of them, the resurrection means only that the dead Jesus continued to live on in the hearts and minds of his followers. Such subjective theories of Christ's resurrection* can become even more elaborate. Daniel Fuller explains Paul Tillich's sub-

**Comments About
the Six Questions**

---

*What I here call a "subjective theory" of Christ's resurrection is one that insists that the essence of the Easter event is what happened and what continues to happen exclusively in the subjective religious experience of believers. While an objective view of the resurrection would not deny the importance of the subjective aspect, it holds that the miracle described in Scripture occurred objectively.

jective theory of the resurrection: "Tillich asserts that the resurrection is nothing more than the awakening in the minds of the disciples after Jesus' death of the 'New Being' that they had seen with such transparency in Jesus before his death."[127] And so the first question that must be asked about any thinker's view of the resurrection is what he understands by the term. What is the essence or meaning of the resurrection?

Attention has already been drawn to the fact that interpretations of the resurrection fall into theories that are either objective or subjective. However, again, the terms *objective* and *subjective* are ambiguous and require some unpacking. George Ladd points out that the word *objective* may mean either that the event in question was *publicly observable* or that *it actually took place in the real world outside of people's subjective consciousness* (that is, it did not simply exist in people's minds or imagination). Not everything that is objective in the second sense of happening in the real world is objective in the first sense of being publicly observable. Ladd illustrates this with a helpful comparison between two statements:[128]

(a) Jesus died.

(b) Jesus died for the sins of the world.

Christians believe that both (a) and (b) are true statements about the crucifixion of Jesus. Both (a) and (b) are objective in the sense that they happened in the real world. Both the death of Jesus and the atonement grounded on his sacrifice were objective in the sense that they happened "out there." But even though both (a) and (b) were objective in one of the above senses, only (a) was objective in the sense of being publicly observable, of being open to public gaze. Anyone present at the scene could have seen Jesus die. But no one standing at the cross, no eyewitness of the crucifixion *saw* Christ's atonement for the sins of the world. The truth of (a), *Jesus died,* was publicly observable. The truth of (b) was not. Statement (a), *Jesus died,* is a straightforward historical claim; but (b), *Jesus died for the sins of the world,* is not so much a historical claim as it is an interpretation or explanation of something that happened in history.

Thus, even though the statement *Jesus died for the sins of the world* is not objective in the sense of its truth being open to public gaze, it is objective in the sense that it really happened in history. The atonement had an invisible dimension, a Godward side, that precluded its being open to public gaze. In order to understand that invisible dimension, men and women need an inspired interpretation that is made available through special revelation.

The two senses of objectivity that we have noted have obvious relevance to the resurrection of Jesus. Is the statement *Jesus rose from the dead* more like *Jesus died* or like *Jesus died for the sins of the world?* That is, was the resurrection, like the atonement, an event that contained a dimension hidden from human eyes? A number of theologians believe it was, a fact that leads them to say that even though the resurrection is objective in the sense that it really happened "out there" in history, it is not objective in the sense that it is or was publicly observable.

The two senses of "objective" that we have noted bring us to the second and third questions to be studied in this chapter.

2. *Did the resurrection occur in the world of space and time?* In other words, is the resurrection objective in the sense that it is not simply something that happened or happens in the mind, religious consciousness, or imagination of people? This leads to the third question.

3. *Was the Resurrection publicly observable?* In other words, was it the sort of event that could have been observed by any eyewitness who happened to be in the right place at the right time?

4. *Is the resurrection verifiable in the same way that other historical events are?* As we have seen, verifying even the most ordinary of historical events can sometimes be a complex task. It will be helpful if complications like this are ignored during the present discussion. The issue here is simply this: If we grant that ordinary historical events can be verified in some way, is it possible for the resurrection to be verified in the same general way?

5. *Does history provide total support, partial sup-*

port, or no support for faith in the resurrection?
Theologians have obviously taken decidedly different
positions with regard to the dependence of faith on
history. Some seem to suggest that faith in an event
like the resurrection is completely dependent on history such that if history should succeed in producing
conclusive "proof" (whatever this might turn out to
mean) that a particular event occurred, faith must
follow automatically. Others swing to the opposite
end of the spectrum and seem to regard faith as totally
immune to any kind of support or attack from history.
A third group thinks the relationship between faith
and history is more complex in the sense that history
can at best provide only partial albeit important support for faith.

6. *Can the resurrection be known apart from history?* Naturally, the question begins with what the
particular thinker means by the Resurrection and then
asks if *that* resurrection can be known only through
history or whether it can be known in some way other
than history.

Now that we have identified the six questions we
will ask, we can begin to notice the answers given to
these questions by Bultmann, Barth, Pannenberg, and
Ladd.

**Bultmann and
the Resurrection**

Bultmann's position on the resurrection of Jesus
seems clearly subjectivist. For Bultmann, the resurrection should not be regarded as something that happened to Jesus in the past. The resurrection is something that happens *within the believer* in his present.
The resurrection is not Jesus' rising from the grave; it
is rather the rise of faith, of a new existential self-
understanding, within us. As Carl Braaten explains,
the essence of Easter faith for Bultmann "is to believe
in the Christ present in the preaching of the church.
This faith does not hinge upon a miraculous event in
history additional to Jesus' death on the cross."[129]

It follows then that for Bultmann the resurrection is
not objective in either of the two senses explained
earlier. For one thing, the resurrection did not happen
in the world of space and time. As Bultmann puts it,

"A historical fact which involves a resurrection from the dead is utterly inconceivable."[130] A few pages later in the same book, he states, "The resurrection itself is not an event of past history."[131] Clearly any "event" that did not occur in the spatio-temporal world would also fail to be publicly observable. Therefore the resurrection, on Bultmann's account, fails to be objective in the second sense as well. Bultmann was not concerned, as Kantzer points out, "with whether or not events described in the Christian gospel actually and literally happened within the framework of human history and in the manner described by biblical statements."[132]

Even though the resurrection never happened as an actual event in space and time for Bultmann, it still retains symbolic significance as an expression of the possibility of a human being's attaining a new and existential self-understanding. The Easter event never happened; but the Easter faith remains a central point in the Christian kerygma. The resurrection is something that happens within our present and not in the past history of Jesus.

As for our fourth question, *Is the resurrection verifiable in the same general way that other historical events are?* Bultmann's answer is an emphatic no! Historical support for the resurrection (the area of our fifth question) is impossible since the resurrection does not belong to the realm of history. Moreover, Bultmann gives an affirmative answer to our last question, *Can the resurrection be known apart from history?* One way in which the resurrection comes to be known is in the preaching of the church. But the most important knowledge of the resurrection occurs within the believer's own religious consciousness. As the believer achieves new levels of self-understanding, he experiences for himself what Bultmann regards as the essence of the resurrection.

The drift of contemporary theology is away from Bultmann's radical disjunction between history and the resurrection. Certainly Barth* and Pannenberg make this feature of Bultmann's thought a major point

---

*This is the later Barth of the *Church Dogmatics*.

of contention. Carl Braaten observes that for theologians like Pannenberg, Gerhard Koch, Richard Reinhold Niebuhr, and others,

> the unity of event and meaning is an indispensable condition for making sense of the accounts of the resurrection, both from a historical and a theological point of view. There is little excuse for pretending eloquence about the meaning of the resurrection while holding reservations about whether the event really happened. The assertion that Jesus was raised from the dead cannot at the same time be theologically true and historically false.[133]

Braaten shows that one need not be an Evangelical to be struck by the radical difference between Bultmann and the apostle Paul:

> Instead of drawing the existentialists' conclusion that faith is especially heroic when taking into itself the utter groundlessness of its affirmations, the apostle Paul did not shrink from admitting that our faith and our preaching are all in vain, "If Christ has not been raised." (I Cor. 15:14). Paul's mention of a list of witnesses indicates that for him, as well as for the apostolic tradition in general, Jesus' resurrection from the dead was an event quite other than faith *in* him. The Easter event includes the apostles' faith, but cannot be reduced to it. The event that establishes faith is the post-Easter appearance of Jesus of Nazareth, who in his exalted mode of being is nevertheless personally identical with the humble form of his earthly existence. The risen Christ was recognized by the disciples as none other than the crucified Jesus.[134]

Some of Bultmann's European critics, such as Paul Althaus, attack him for turning the gospel into an entirely subjective matter. Althaus sees Bultmann's thought, not as a contemporary restatement of Pauline justification by faith, but as a contemporary extension of the liberal feeling-theology of Schleiermacher.*

---

*See Paul Althaus, *Fact and Faith in the Kerygma of Today,* trans. David Cairns (Philadelphia: Muhlenberg, 1960), pp. 54, 82. Friedrich Schleiermacher (1768–1834), a professor at the University of Berlin, was a formative influence on Protestant liberalism. Some of the details of this influence are traced in Ronald Nash, *The Word of God and the Mind of Man* (Grand Rapids: Zondervan, 1982), chap. 2.

In America, liberal scholar Schubert Ogden has followed Bultmann in holding that a bodily resurrection of Jesus "would be just as relevant to my salvation as an existing self or person as that the carpenter next door just drove a nail in a two-by-four, or that American technicians have at last been successful in recovering a nose cone that had first been placed in orbit around the earth."[135] Ogden's shockingly blunt way of making his point demonstrates clearly the chasm separating him and Bultmann from the world of the New Testament writers and the thought of historic Christianity. Carl Braaten rejects the position of Bultmann and Ogden for promoting a New Testament that "is not only demythologized, not only dehistorized, but also to the last degree dekerygmatized. All that remains is a humanistic philosophy of existence that finally has no need of the New Testament or the resurrection of Jesus Christ."[136] Braaten has good reason for objecting to Bultmann's reinterpretation of the New Testament resurrection texts as an expression of a new human self-understanding:

> However, there is nothing that more directly contravenes the "intention" of these texts than to read them merely as expressions of a new self-understanding. Where is the evidence that the authors of these texts were primarily interested in expressing their new understanding of existence? . . . . For the meaning of the Easter proclamation has its center of gravity not in the faith which receives, but in the event which makes the faith of Easter a possibility in the first place. The resurrection event is God's act of exalting Jesus beyond the nihility of death. Without this event having really occurred, there is no existential core of meaning in the resurrection stories worth talking about. The basis of the church's proclamation would thereby be removed and the content of its faith evacuated of all meaning.[137]

Anyone who takes the New Testament seriously, then, will look past the views of Bultmann and his followers for an adequate account of the relationship between history and the resurrection.

**Barth and the
Resurrection**

In some ways, the earlier position taken by Karl Barth* with respect to history was even more radical than that held at the time by Bultmann.[138] In the 1933 edition of his commentary on Romans, Barth argued that Paul's words in 1 Corinthians 15:1–11 were not offered as historical evidence for the resurrection but only as articles of faith testifying to the miracle of God's self-disclosure to man. With the passage of time, however, Barth's attitude toward history changed.[139] He reached a point where he criticized Bultmann for denying the objectivity of the resurrection and turning it into something entirely subjective. For Barth, the one who actually rose from the dead was the same Jesus the disciples had known in the flesh.[140] The development that took place in Barth's thought makes it more difficult to discern his answers to our six questions. The *early* Barth (the Barth of the 1920s and early 1930s) denigrated history in favor of some type of superhistory. However, the Barth of the *Church Dogmatics,* in spite of occasional lapses that appear to be reversions to his earlier position, came to affirm the view that the resurrection was objective in the sense that it was an event that took place in the real world of space and time. The resurrection as well as the postresurrection appearances of Jesus really happened "out there" (Question 2).[141] But even though the later Barth regarded the resurrection as objective in the sense that it happened in space and time, he did *not* think it was objective in the sense of being *publicly observable* (Question 3). Nor did Barth think the resurrection *verifiable* in the same way that other historical events are (Question 4). In

---

*The passage of time will undoubtedly show that Karl Barth was this century's most important theologian. Born in Switzerland in 1886, Barth was trained in the prevailing liberal theology. But when his liberal presuppositions were shattered by World War I, Barth turned to the Bible. At first, he advocated a neoorthodox theology that contained a heavy dose of existentialist philosophy. His multivolumed *Church Dogmatics* represented a major break with existentialism as he sought to hear and proclaim the Word of God contained in the Bible. Barth's relevance for evangelical theology is disputed by American Evangelicals. See Gregory G. Bolich, *Karl Barth and Evangelicalism* (Downers Grove, Ill.: InterVarsity, 1980).

fact, he refused to allow that the resurrection might be verified by historical investigation (Question 5).[142] The resurrection event described in the Gospels was an event that history cannot understand, even though it occurred within history. Even though the resurrection was an event in history, it is not knowable by historical means (Question 6). It is difficult to know precisely what Barth meant by the word *history*. Some people doubt that Barth himself could have defined the term as he used it. While he no longer had some kind of superhistory in view, Barth's "history" cannot be equated with the history studied and written by historians.

Barth's answers to the six questions, then, are as follows: What is the essence of the resurrection? God's raising Jesus from the dead. Did the resurrection occur in the world of space and time? Yes. Was it publicly observable? No. Is it verifiable by ordinary historical investigation? No. Can it be known by some means other than history? Yes. In fact, it can be known *only by some nonhistorical means*.[143] For Barth, the Spirit of God creates assurance within believers that God really did raise Jesus from the dead. But no historical knowledge or verification of the resurrection is possible. Does history provide any support for the resurrection? None at all. For Barth, the resurrection is a revelatory event. Since Barth thinks that revelation is always salvational and is always God's speaking to man, any cognitive component of divine revelation must always take a subordinate place to the salvational. As Kantzer explains, "The Spirit of God—alone and as a work of pure divine grace—creates in us the assurance that God really did enter the stream of human history, to become incarnate in Jesus Christ, to die on the cross for our sins, and to rise again from the dead for our salvation."[144] But as Kantzer adds, this raises serious problems as Barth "seeks to extract historical truth and the assurance of historical facts out of a subjective experience."[145] Therefore *Barth like Bultmann seems to hold that faith can receive no support or help from history*. For Barth, faith in the resurrection depends on Jesus' making himself known immediately in our present experience. Left unanswered by Barth is how one's knowledge of a historical event can be derived exclusively from a work of God in the human soul. Certainly, Daniel Fuller observes, Barth is drastically out of step with the New Testament:

> The apostolic witness is a fact of history, and faith must ever render respect to it. So long as the resurrection appearances led to the historical event of the apostolic witness to this fact, it is impossible to ignore this intermediate witness and declare that knowledge of the resurrection comes only from an immediate revelation of Christ himself. Thus in connection with the question of the apostolic witness, Barth finds it necessary to make a statement that opens the door to knowledge of the resurrection gained by the historical method. Hence there remains in Barth an unreconciled tension between faith and the historical method.[146]

Some writers have discussed the apparent similarity between Barth's position and the earlier view of German scholar Hans von Campenhausen. Campenhausen had also stressed the fact that faith in the resurrection is the result of a work of God in the soul rather than a result of historical reasoning. In Campenhausen's words:

> The dry historical data, which we can ascertain, are by no means a sufficient reproduction of the fullness of the resurrection message of primitive Christianity. This message cannot be understood without auxiliary and illuminating interpretation of the events and without an unfolding of that power that makes a claim upon one and imparts to the historical events their full meaning. . . . The credibility of the Easter message does not rest upon strictly historical proofs, but rather . . . upon the existential verification of the Spirit. . . .[147]

However much they may disagree on other matters, both Barth and Campenhausen advance a resurrection faith that history can neither strengthen nor weaken. If Campenhausen, for one,

> were to leave this middle ground and seek to explain why the tomb was empty and why the disciples thought they saw Jesus, the result would be a natural or supernatural explanation and faith would then be either supported or countered by history. But because Campenhausen does

not follow the usual historical procedure and seek after the causes for these facts [such as the empty tomb], it seems that his reconstruction is not so much history as theology. Therefore it appears that history, if it were allowed to speak freely would have something to say for or against faith. Thus Campenhausen, despite his attempt to construct a history that is impartial to faith, succeeds actually in showing, like Barth . . . , that faith cannot have a knowledge of the resurrection which can remain unaffected by the apostolic witness and the historical method.[148]

Barth's attempt at a mediating position that clings to history with one hand while throwing it away with the other wilts under careful scrutiny. This is one fence that cannot be straddled. One must either jump to the left and end up in Bultmann's lap or else jump to the right and affirm that history is relevant to faith in the resurrection. Many people believe that Wolfhart Pannenberg's position, which we will examine now, provides the proper corrective to the views of Barth and Bultmann.

Pannenberg and the Resurrection

Some care must be exercised when approaching Pannenberg's view of the resurrection, for things are not always as they seem. Pannenberg *seems to affirm* a dogmatic position with regard to the factual historicity of Christ's bodily resurrection from the dead. His answers to our six questions are commonly thought to be as follows: (1) the resurrection means Christ's bodily resurrection from the dead. (2) The resurrection was objective in the sense that it took place in the world of space and time. (3) The resurrection was also objective in the sense that it was, in principle, publicly observable. Had any human eyewitness been in the right place at the right time, he could have observed the resurrection. (4) The resurrection is verifiable in the same way that other historical events are. (5) History can provide total support for belief in the resurrection. (6) The resurrection cannot be known in any way other than through history. I repeat: these propositions express what is commonly believed to be Pannenberg's position on the resurrection of Christ.

Certainly Pannenberg regards the resurrection as the central event of the Christian faith. He believes that only a historical resurrection can explain the sudden transformation of the disciples and the survival of the early Christian community. Without the empty tomb, the Jewish enemies of Christianity would have had an unanswerable refutation of the early Christian preaching.

Bultmann denigrated the historicity of the resurrection in favor of a faith that arises within the believer from hearing the Christian message. Barth, though allowing for the historicity of the resurrection event, regarded history as impotent either to provide knowledge of or to produce faith in the event because such a faith could arise only from the inward testimony of the Holy Spirit. Pannenberg is often thought to have gone to the other extreme by making faith in the resurrection arise solely from knowledge of what occurred in history. In other words, Pannenberg is supposed to be an objectivist with regard to the resurrection, Bultmann is a subjectivist, and Barth tried unsuccessfully to find a resting place somewhere between the two.

Writing in his book, *Faith and Reality,* Pannenberg declares that "Christian faith would be in a bad state if the resurrection of Jesus were not really an historical fact. Moreover, as Paul insisted, our faith would be vain. . . . there is today no conclusive objection against assuming that Jesus' resurrection is an historical fact."[149] Pannenberg expresses his deep regret over the drift of recent theology away from some objective and historical moorings for Christian faith:

> Because of the apparent danger to the foundations of faith from historical research, theology has allowed itself in the last fifty years to be forced into taking a disastrous short-cut. An attempt has been made to find a sheltered area, where faith would be independent of historical investigations. Jesus' history has been described as "super-history," "salvation history" or "primal history," as opposed to "ordinary history."[150]

Pannenberg seems clearly to have separated himself from those who like Barth would require a special act of revealing grace in order for human beings to see

God's acts in history. "In distinction from special manifestations of the diety, the historical revelation is open to anyone who has eyes to see. It has a universal character."[151] However, in spite of Pannenberg's strong endorsement of the historical objectivity of events like the resurrection, his total position raises several questions. One major reason why Pannenberg stresses divine revelation in history is that he denigrates divine special revelation in a medium like the Bible.

Whereas Barth emphasized the immediate character of divine revelation, Pannenberg counters by declaring that revelation always comes to human beings through a particular medium, namely, the events of history. This history through which revelation becomes known is not some kind of superhistory or salvation history; it is regular, ordinary history knowable in the same general way as other historical events. Prior faith is not a necessary condition for discerning God's revelation in history. On the contrary, faith arises from an open-minded investigation of events like the resurrection. But as we have noted, Pannenberg is forced to emphasize history as a medium of revelation because of his doubts about Scripture as a medium of revelation.

Pannenberg's belief that history is both a necessary and a sufficient condition for faith gives rise to other problems. For one thing, some are troubled by the fact that Pannenberg's position requires "that only those can have an immediate knowledge of revelation who are trained historians. . . ."[152] This seems to imply that ordinary people are dependent "upon the theologian-historian to provide their basis for faith."[153] An analogy from the history of philosophy may help make this objection clearer. During the Middle Ages, Thomas Aquinas gave direction to much subsequent Catholic thought by introducing a radical disjunction between philosophy (reason) and theology (faith). According to Aquinas, with the one exception of the existence of God, truth about every other matter can be known either by reason (man's unaided rational faculties) or by faith (divinely given revelation). Suppose (and the supposition is contrary to fact) that Aquinas had also stipulated that a knowledge of God's existence is exclusively a matter for reason and not faith. Had Aquinas advanced this view, it would have entailed the absurd conclusion that ordinary people would be totally dependent on philosophers to provide their basis for belief in God's existence. But as we know, most people who believe in the existence of God are totally indifferent to the arguments of the philosophers. By analogy, Pannennberg seems to place the common man at the mercy of the historian so far as his knowledge of the resurrection is concerned, when the simple fact is that millions of Christians around the world believe in the resurrection without any actual help from the historians.

To make things worse, it is difficult to know how, given Pannenberg's view, it is possible for any person having an adequate understanding of the historical evidence to continue in a state of unbelief. Surely, some begging of the question is involved in any suggestion that people who refuse to believe simply don't know all the facts or have not approached the evidence with a sufficiently open mind. If historical evidence is a sufficient condition for faith in the resurrection, anyone knowing the evidence would be compelled to believe. Pannenberg seems unaware that in addition to objective evidence and valid argumentation, something must take place *subjectively* to *produce* faith. Faith is a response to objective truth and the subjective working of the Holy Spirit.

But perhaps the basic reason why Pannenberg's position must be rejected is that he, like so many others we have noticed, denies all possibility of supernaturalism. Pannenberg cannot believe that God might be revealed only in some historical events and be revealed only to special groups like the Christian church or Israel. For Pannenberg, either all of history reveals God or none of it does. But that appears to leave Pannenberg without an answer to the indisputable fact that while some believe, many who have access to the same information do not. Pannenberg's theory is in clear opposition to the biblical view that at different times and places, God reveals Himself in a special way to selected individuals or groups. Pannenberg rejects this so-called two-story theory of history on the ground that it would rule out the possibility of historical knowledge about anything. He cannot imagine how the historical method could begin to obtain knowledge about what transpires on the second story of the universe. But he conveniently ignores the problems he has explaining how the historical method operates on his one level of history.

Evangelical critics of Pannenberg are right, then, in maintaining that Pannenberg's approach to history must be corrected to include the recognition that God does intervene supernaturally within history in special ways to particular people. Once this assumption is granted, Daniel Fuller explains,

> there is no difficulty in understanding how only the nation of Israel came to its particular view of history: God simply intervened in her milieu and not in any other. Then, too, there is no difficulty in understanding why some do not believe the revelation mediated by history: God simply does not work supernaturally in the heart of everyone who hears the Gospel in order to overcome their prejudices so that they might own up to the truth of what is to be known in history. To understand the Holy Spirit as intervening specially in the behalf of certain people so that they acknowledge the truth mediated by history is not to deny that revelation is mediated solely through history. The work of the Holy Spirit would be conceived of as enabling a man to own up to what was already to be seen in history, rather than supplementing it in any way.[154]

So far we have examined, without satisfaction, three major approaches to the relationship between the resurrection and history. As the defects of each theory have become clear, the outline of what an adequate theory must contain has become more apparent. It is time to see if an evangelical approach holds more promise.

George Ladd and the Resurrection

Before George Ladd's answers to our six questions can be noted, a fairly detailed exposition of his treatment of the resurrection is necessary. Ladd is confident that the miracle of the resurrection occurred, that Christ rose triumphant from the dead, and that his resurrection occurred in the world of space and time. Even though Ladd holds that the resurrection was objective in the sense that it happened "out there," he stops short of allowing the resurrection to be objective in the second sense, that is, as a publicly observable event. Moreover, Ladd refuses to allow that the resurrection is verifiable in the same way that other historical events are verifiable. Ladd's reasons for all of this must be examined.

For one thing, Ladd explains, there were no actual eyewitnesses to the resurrection itself. There were eyewitnesses to the empty tomb and plenty of eyewitnesses to the postresurrection appearances of Christ. But at the actual moment of the resurrection, no human eyewitness was inside the tomb to observe the event itself (Mark 16:14; Luke 24:2; John 20:2). But, someone might ask, doesn't the really important question at this point concern whether the resurrection was publicly observable *in principle?* Granted that no one was in the tomb when the resurrection occurred, isn't it true that if someone had been, he or she would have been an eyewitness? Ladd answers this question in the negative. Even if there had been eyewitnesses inside the tomb at the moment of the resurrection, there is nothing they would have seen. Ladd's reason for saying this is his belief that the resurrection of Jesus was not simply a revivification of Jesus' corpse. "The fact of the matter is," Ladd writes, "the resurrection is not the return of Jesus to physical earthly life, but it is the event in which Jesus passed from earthly, mortal existence into the realm of immortality."[155] This means that

> something happened to the body of Jesus, giving it new and marvellous powers. The body emerged from the grave clothes without disturbing them, leaving them intact. Obviously, Jesus had not *revived*. Obviously, the body had not been stolen. It has simply disappeared.[156]

Any potential eyewitness who might have been present inside the tomb at the moment of resurrection would not have seen a dead body return to life. All that this person would have "seen" was the body of Jesus suddenly disappear. A disappearing body and a person rising from the dead are different phenomena, even though they may be part of the same event.

Our first question regarding the resurrection concerns what the thinker in question means by the resurrection. It is clear then that Ladd thinks the resurrection cannot be defined simply as the revivification of Jesus' dead body. Rather, as already noted, the resurrection "is the event in which Jesus passed from earthly, mortal existence into the realm of immortality."[157] Ladd's view does *not entail doubts about the event being a bodily resurrection.* Careful attention needs to be given to what Paul wrote in 1 Corinthians 15 about the differences between the earthly and physical body and the resurrection body. Ladd insists that the risen Christ was a real person in a real body, albeit a body endowed with remarkable powers. Jesus' postresurrection appearances were "in tangible, visible, bodily form."[158]

Ladd's position requires a more careful analysis of the significance of the empty tomb than one often finds in some conservative discussions of the resurrection. If Ladd's approach to the resurrection is sound,

> it should become clear that witnessing the resurrection would of itself be no proof of the resurrection. [Ladd means here the disappearance of Christ's body in the tomb.] It would be only a bewildering event which would leave the disciples in confusion, wondering what marvellous thing had happened. The [post-resurrection] appearances were necessary to convince the disciples that Jesus was really alive from the dead. The empty tomb did not prove this, as we have seen [Peter saw the empty tomb but did not believe]. The empty tomb was, however, a witness to the *nature* of the resurrection. It was not a "resurrection of Jesus' spirit," but a resurrection of his body.[159]

Still another reason behind Ladd's approach to the resurrection is his analysis of miracles and their relation to history. Ladd makes it clear that he believes in miracles; it is also clear that he regards the resurrection as a miracle. Ladd objects strenuously to the naturalistic presuppositions that pervade the world views of thinkers like Bultmann. Whatever else a miracle may be, it is an act of God. It is an act or event in which eternity breaks into time. But this leads Ladd to say, "A miracle is an event *in history* which has *no historical cause*. It is an act of God, not of man."[160] For Ladd, historians can investigate only those historical events that have causes that themselves are within history. But this means, on his account, that even though a miracle may happen within history, its cause (God) is outside of history. Thus, even though Ladd acknowledges the historicity of the resurrection, "its nature is such that it cannot be explained by the ordinary historical laws of cause and effect. Every 'historical' event must have a 'historical' cause. The resurrection of Jesus was an act of God, unmediated by any other historical event."[161] In other words, "the resurrection was a *real event* in past history but whose nature is such that it transcends history and therefore is not subject to strict verification."[162]

Like every other miracle, the resurrection has a dimension beyond history. Its cause (God) is outside of history; it is a case of transcendence intervening in history. But though there is a transhistorical dimension to the resurrection, the resurrection itself is not a simple historical event. The very nature of the resurrection as miracle takes it outside the ordinary realm of cause and effect, which are the proper province of historical investigation. The historian qua historian doesn't know what to do with a miracle, an event that has a cause outside of history.

To summarize the discussion to this point, Ladd insists that the resurrection is objective in the sense that it really happened in history. But it is not objective in the sense that it was open to public gaze. While the postresurrection appearances were objective in this second sense, the actual resurrection itself was not. What is Ladd's answer to our fourth question, Is the resurrection verifiable in the same way that other historical events are? His answer might be both yes and no. Some things related to the resurrection are verifiable in an ordinary historical way: there is important secondary support for the resurrection in eyewitness testimony to the empty tomb, the post-resurrection appearances, and so on. Even though no one saw Jesus rise from the dead, there is plenty of circumstantial evidence that, understood properly, can lead to faith in the resurrection. This includes the undisturbed grave clothes, the sealed tomb, the empty tomb, etc. Therefore, adequate eyewitness testimony to circumstantial evidence that has the resurrection as its most plausible hypothesis is available. But the resurrection itself (Jesus' actual passage into immortality) is not verifiable in the same way that other historical events are.

Does Ladd believe that history can provide total, partial, or no support for belief in the resurrection? His answer seems to be *partial support*.

> It is not possible for historical criticism to *prove* the resurrection. It is the task of anti-criticism to establish that there are no known historical facts which contradict the Easter faith. In other words, the *hypothesis* that Jesus actually rose from the dead is the best hypothesis to account for the known historical facts. . . . It is not the purpose of this book therefore by historical reasoning to prove the resurrection. It is our purpose to establish the thesis that the bodily resurrection of Christ is the only adequate explanation to account for the resurrection faith and the admitted 'historical' facts. Thus we hope to show that, for one who believes in the God who has revealed himself in Christ, the resurrection is entirely rational and utterly consistent with the evidences.[163]

The reason why history can provide only partial support for the resurrection is that *some aspects of it are historically verifiable and some are not*. In the final analysis, our assent to the resurrection must involve both history and faith. There will always be an aspect of the resurrection that transcends what history can discover and prove.

The fact that the historical evidence for the resurrection is circumstantial does not weaken the case for the resurrection, and here is where many misunderstand. Many criminal law cases are such that the only available evidence is circumstantial but still compelling. Such is the case with the resurrection.

One of the more important pieces of circumstantial evidence was the disciples' belief that Christ had risen.

> The disciples *believed* that they had seen Jesus alive after his death. They *believed* in the bodily resurrection of Jesus. Here we are on bedrock. It is impossible to question the facticity of the disciple's belief in Jesus' resurrection. What is the *historical* cause of this faith? What historical event caused them to believe that Jesus had risen from the dead?[164]

One task of the historian is to explain significant events in the past. One such event is the belief of the early church that Christ had risen. What best explains this belief? Speaking for all those who believe, Alan Richardson writes, "All of the evidence . . . points to the judgment that the Church did not create the belief in the resurrection of Christ; the resurrection of Christ, historically speaking, created the Church by calling faith into being."[165] Only the *actual resurrection* of Christ is sufficient to explain the faith of the early disciples and the origin, growth, and spread of the Christian religion.

Conclusion

It will be helpful to summarize the discussion of this chapter with a chart that gives the answers of these four theologians to each of our six questions.

1. What is the essence or meaning of the resurrection?

> BULTMANN: the rise of a new existential self-awareness within believers
> BARTH: God's raising Jesus from the dead
> PANNENBERG: Christ's bodily resurrection from the dead
> LADD: the passage of Jesus from earthly, mortal existence into the realm of immortality, an event that includes his bodily resurrection

2. Did the resurrection happen in space and time?

> BULTMANN: no
> BARTH: yes

PANNENBERG: yes
LADD: yes

133

History and the
Resurrection
of Christ

3. Was the resurrection publicly observable?

> BULTMANN: no
> BARTH: no
> PANNENBERG: yes
> LADD: yes and no. What was publicly observable
> is circumstantial evidence such as the empty
> tomb. The actual event was not.

4. Is the resurrection verifiable in the same way that other events are?

> BULTMANN: no
> BARTH: no
> PANNENBERG: yes
> LADD: yes and no. The strong circumstantial evidence that supports belief in the resurrection can be verified in normal historical ways. But the actual event is not open to this typical kind of verification.

5. What kind of support does history provide for belief in the resurrection?

> BULTMANN: none
> BARTH: none
> PANNENBERG: total (?)
> LADD: partial

6. Can the resurrection be known apart from history?

> BULTMANN: yes
> BARTH: yes
> PANNENBERG: no
> LADD: yes, if one refers to the circumstantial evidence; no, if one refers to the resurrection event itself.

Ladd's discussion of the resurrection and its relation to history avoids the vagueness that characterizes many treatments of the subject. It would not be surprising—if Barth were able and if Pannenberg were willing to comment on the details of Ladd's exposition—if both Barth and Pannenberg clarified their positions on some points to accord more closely with Ladd's view. In Barth's case, all one can do is speculate. Bultmann, I remain confident, would not alter his view.

Of the four sets of answers to our six questions about the resurrection, the position of Ladd is more at home with the total New Testament teaching about the resurrection and with the demand that faith in the resurrection maintain a respectable relationship to history. Those who disallow any role for historical reasoning in providing support for faith in Christ's resurrection ought to be embarrassed; obviously they don't quite know what to do with the apostolic witness to the resurrection, which is not only itself a historical record but which must be treated using the methods of historical investigation. Those who cut themselves off from any historical evidence or support for the resurrection must, if they are to be consistent, also ignore the Gospel record as a witness to the resurrection.

chapter eight

Faith and History

The relationship between faith and history is examined. This examination is based on Norman Perrin's distinction between historical, historic, and faith-knowledge. The place of faith in any kind of historical knowledge is further developed.

At first glance, answering the question of how personal faith is related to history seems relatively easy. It might appear that all one has to do is make a choice among three options:

1. faith is dependent on history
2. faith is independent of history
3. some mediating option, if it exists.

While some people operate at a level at which they are satisfied with affirming, let us say, that *faith is dependent on history,* the claim needs to be unpacked. As different meanings are assigned to the words *faith, depend,* and *history,* the apparently simple claim can express a number of different theories.

135

One helpful way to work through a difficult subject like the relationship between personal faith and history is to use an earlier discussion of the topic as a starting point. Our starting point will be a view quite different from mine, namely, that advanced by Norman Perrin[166] Perrin's distinction between three kinds of knowledge (historical knowledge, historic knowledge, and faith knowledge)* will be used as a basis for my own discussion of the dependence or independence of faith and history.

Perrin's *historical knowledge* is the kind of knowledge about the past provided by scientific historiography (that is, post-Enlightenment historiography). This would be the kind of historical knowledge illustrated by Ranke's quest for history "as it really was." Perrin describes historical knowledge as "hard knowledge." By this he means that such knowledge is sought *apart from* any possible utility it might have for later generations and *apart from* any special interest or lack of interest that the researcher might have in it. Historical knowledge is objective in the sense that it is open to critical revision in the light of new information.

Historic knowledge, Perrin explains, "is essentially a selection from the collection of 'hard' historical knowledge. Some of this knowledge will be found to be directly significant, in various ways, to a man of today."[167] In other words, later generations cull from the large mass of historical knowledge available to them information that is relevant or significant for them personally or for their contemporaries. For example, the Academy Award-winning movie of 1981, *Chariots of Fire,* contained much historical knowledge about the Scottish runner and missionary, Eric Liddell, who won a gold medal at the 1924 Olympics.† Many people have found Liddell's refusal

---

*Perrin's distinction between historical and historic knowledge has some dependence on Martin Kähler's well-known distinction between the historical Jesus and the historic Jesus, between the Jesus of *Historie* and the Jesus of *Geschichte.*

†People who have studied Liddell's life know that some things in the screen play were fictionalized to enhance the dramatic appeal of the story. Some aspects of the film narrative were not *Historie.*

to compromise his Christian convictions so inspirational that they have been brought to new levels of Christian commitment in their own lives. In this way, historical knowledge has become historic knowledge, has assumed existential significance. The basic difference between historical and historic knowledge is the importance, significance, relevance, and meaningfulness that some historical knowledge will have for some later generation that treats it as historic.* "Historical knowledge from the past becomes directly significant, that is, it becomes historic knowledge, to us in our present, in so far as it 'speaks to our condition', 'has a direct point of contact with us', or the like."[168] Of all the past events important enough to be included in *Historie,* some assume sufficient significance to be included in some later generation's *Geschichte.* Historic knowledge differs from historical knowledge in the degree of its importance for a particular thinker or group of thinkers.

In addition to historical and historic knowledge, Perrin introduces a third category he calls *"faith-knowledge."* To paraphrase Anselm, faith knowledge is that knowledge about the past that is so important that no more important knowledge can be conceived. Perrin makes the following claims about faith knowledge.

1. *Faith knowledge is inseparable from religious commitment.* Whereas some kind of neutrality is both possible and desirable in the cases of historical and historic knowledge, neutrality is impossible with re-

---

*In order to avoid a possible misunderstanding, Perrin's contrast between historical and historic knowledge requires some amplification. Perrin's distinction appears to conflict with the important insight, noted early in this book, that history is concerned *only* with important things that happened in the past. Unless a past event was important or believed to be important, it would not have been preserved in any historical record. Perrin's teaching can be preserved if we relate it to a threefold distinction: (1) the simple past, which includes all of the past that is too trivial to be preserved in any historical record; (2) the important past, which includes everything so preserved (I identify Perrin's historical knowledge with this second type); and (3) the *important* important past, namely, "hard information" about the past that becomes significant for some later generation. This would be Perrin's historic knowledge.

gard to faith knowledge. Faith knowledge becomes possible only when religious faith or commitment enters the picture. This commitment may be either that of some believing individual or that of a community of believers.

2. Perrin seems to hold that *faith knowledge is restricted to faith in Jesus Christ.* Apparently for Perrin, only one set of historic circumstances is sufficient to bring people to faith knowledge:

> "Faith-knowledge" depends upon special worth being attributed to the person concerned, so that knowledge of that person assumes a significance beyond the historic. Historic significance can be attributed to almost any number of people from the past . . . but "faith-knowledge" could be attributed only to the one figure who comes to be of special significance in terms of revelation, religious experience, religious belief.[169]

"Jesus died" is an item of historical knowledge; but it is also a piece of historic knowledge. The death of Jesus was an event both momentous and significant, not only in our own experience but for that of the entire human race. But by faith knowledge, one recognizes an added dimension in the picture of Jesus so that that person can affirm, "Jesus died for *my* sins." The historic knowledge about Jesus' death assumes a value beyond that which we could ascribe to any other individual in history. "Christ died for my sins," Perrin states, is a declaration of faith knowledge and not historical knowledge.

> The value here ascribed to that death [of Jesus] is not ascribed to it because of what Jesus did, but because of what God is regarded as having done. . . . That Jesus died nobly or showed confidence in God are [*sic*] historical statements, subject to the vicissitudes of historical research, but that his death fulfilled the purpose of God in regard to "my sins" is certainly not such a statement, and it lies beyond the power of the historian even to consider it, even though, as a Christian, he might believe it.[170]

What Perrin has pointed out is that while the *statement* "Jesus died" *can be investigated historically,* the claim "Jesus died for the sins of the world" is a *theological interpretation* of the historical event *that transcends* historical research. The reason why we have faith knowledge is not just that we know Jesus died but that we come to see something more in his death than the simple execution of a human being. The historian can in principle verify the fact that Jesus died; but in his capacity as historian he cannot investigate the further claim that Jesus died for my sins. This adds a *transhistorical dimension* to the death of Jesus that lies beyond the purview of the historian.

3. Perrin's first two points about faith knowledge do not seem objectionable to Christians more traditional than he. Many more traditional theologians, however, will object to his third claim: *Faith knowledge has no necessary dependence on historical knowledge.* At this point in Perrin's discussion, two questions become relevant. First, can an event (or the story of an event) be the object of historic knowledge without it also belonging to the class of historical knowledge? Can something be *Geschichte* (meaningful) without also being *Historie* (actual)? And second, can an event (or story of that event) be an object of faith knowledge without it also being *Historie?* Many, including Bultmann and Perrin, suggest that both questions can be answered in the affirmative. What is more surprising is that a conservative thinker like I. Howard Marshall also suggests that *Geshichte* is not necessarily dependent on *Historie.*[171] We have noted the philosophical and theological presuppositions that explain the ease with which Bultmann divorces *Geschichte* and *Historie.* Marshall's reasons are quite different, as is the nature of the separation in his thought. Marshall is struck by the empirical fact that people often do believe in stories about historical personages that historical research shows never happened. Americans, for example, believe in a number of stories about national heroes like Washington and Lincoln that are legend. And so, Marshall concludes, myth or legend can become an object of faith knowledge; we can have faith knowledge about either real or imaginary events and people. A story that has become *Geschichte* (assumed existential significance for subsequent generations) may have no actual basis in *Historie.*

An example may help illustrate this. One of the most beautiful and historic sites in England is the ruins of Glastonbury Abbey. Anyone who has visited the ruins can undoubtedly remember standing before what was once the high altar of the abbey, looking down on an apparent grave marked with a sign identifying the spot as the grave of King Arthur. For anyone with even a touch of Romanticism, such an experience can conjure a wealth of feelings. Images of Arthur, the Round Table, and Excalibur can easily force their way into such a person's consciousness at such a time. Even though it is possible that none of the stories about King Arthur have any basis in *Historie,* they can still function as *Geschichte.*

However, it would be a mistake to allow the acceptance of unhistorical legends about a King Arthur or Abraham Lincoln to lead us to ignore an important truth about the relationship between *Geschichte* and *Historie.* If we ignore romantic day-dreaming or heroic legends that have become an important part of a nation's mythology, nonhistorical events that have assumed the status of *Geschichte* have done so because people *believed* them to be historical. As much of a Romantic as I may sometimes be, it would be difficult for me to treat any of the stories about King Arthur as *Geschichte* if I did not believe they had some basis in *Historie.* If I were to stand before Arthur's "grave" completely convinced that he had never existed and that all the stories about him were pure fiction, I could not *rationally* possess any historic knowledge about him. Apart from the belief that some of the stories about Arthur had some basis in *Historie,* romantic daydreaming about him would be indistinguishable from reflections about Snow White and the Seven Dwarfs.

A proper evaluation of Perrin's claim that myth or legend can become the object of faith knowledge requires a distinction between a *descriptive* and a *normative* account of faith. If we look at what people believe from a purely descriptive viewpoint, we find that people as a matter of fact believe all sorts of things for all kinds of reasons, good and bad. In this *descriptive* sense, some people can have faith knowledge in stories that are little more than myths or legends. But this is hardly the point Perrin was concerned to make. Acts of faith knowledge can also be examined *normatively* with a view to discovering what people ought to believe, what they have a right to believe. Such a prescriptive view of faith would take into account what *ought to be* the grounds for a well-formed faith. And so, even though some people may have faith knowledge in that which is not historical, the proper question is, *Should they have such faith knowledge?* As soon as a rational person pinches himself and remembers that none of the stories about King Arthur may be historical, his romantic daydreaming ends and he comes back to reality. Likewise, faith knowledge about Jesus that is knowingly not grounded on historical knowledge cannot qualify as genuine or well-formed faith.

4. Perrin continues by claiming that *faith knowledge is interpersonal.* Using the well-known terminology of Jewish philosopher Martin Buber, we may say that historical and historic knowledge are both examples of I-It knowledge, while faith knowledge is a species of I-Thou knowledge. Buber developed this rather awkward terminology to distinguish between acts of knowledge in which what we know is some *object* or thing and the more personal kind of knowledge in which what we know is some *subject.* For example, my knowledge of this book or my car is I-It knowledge in which I am related to some impersonal thing. But my knowledge of my daughter is I-Thou knowledge in which I am related to another subject. I-Thou knowledge has an existential interpersonal character, which, Perrin thinks, characterizes faith knowledge.

5. Finally, Perrin declares that *faith knowledge is transhistorical.* He expands this point by identifying three ways in which faith knowledge is transhistorical: (1) It is transhistorical because it introduces the idea of a being (God) who transcends history while acting within history. (2) Faith knowledge is transhistorical because it may be independent of both historical and historic knowledge. (3) Finally, faith knowledge is transhistorical because it looks to an

eschatological future; that is, it looks beyond history to the end of history.

To summarize the ground covered thus far, we are examining the relationship between personal faith and history. As a way into our problem, we are building on the start made by Norman Perrin in his distinction between historical knowledge, historic knowledge, and faith knowledge. Perrin's discussion contains many insights that thinkers far more conservative than he can accept. One major disagreement concerns Perrin's readiness to grant validity to faith knowledge that is not grounded on historical or historic knowledge. The existential theology of thinkers like Bultmann and Perrin touches base with convictions of the old Protestant liberalism at several points, one of them being a mutual interest in deemphasizing the place of theoretical knowledge in religion and replacing it with existential commitment or interpersonal communication. An informed Christian orthodoxy does not wish to minimize the subject side (commitment) of Christian belief. But traditional Christianity recognizes that subjective commitment does not exist in a cognitive vacuum. Why does the death of Jesus assume the existential significance it has for faith knowledge? Certainly one reason for its significance is the knowledge human beings can attain of the divine interpretation of the event. As human beings come to understand the proper interpretation of Jesus' death (an interpretation given in special revelation), they reach a place where they understand the need for and the nature of the faith-response appropriate to God's act in Christ. In other words, understanding, interpretation, and cognitive knowledge (as opposed to interpersonal knowledge) are important conditions of faith knowledge missing from Perrin's account.

Perrin continues his discussion of the relationship between faith and history by stating that historical knowledge is relevant to faith knowledge in at least three ways. First, historical knowledge is related *positively* in the sense that it provides content for faith knowledge.

Historical knowledge of Jesus, then, is significant to faith in that it can contribute to the formation of the faith-image. In a tradition which "believes in Jesus", historical knowledge can be a source for the necessary content of faith. After all, in the Christian use, faith is necessarily faith *in* something, a believer believes *in* something, and in so far as that "something" is "Jesus", historical knowledge can help to provide the content, without thereby becoming the main source of that content. The main source will always be the proclamation of the Church, a proclamation arising out of a Christian experience of the risen Lord.[172]

In this paragraph, Perrin is trying to reduce the size of the gap he had earlier posited between faith and historical knowledge. Historical knowledge, it turns out, is important to faith knowledge after all. But it can never be the main source of faith's content; in typical Bultmannian fashion, Perrin locates that main source in the kerygma of the church that may or may not be grounded on historical knowledge.

Second, Perrin indicates that historical knowledge is related to faith knowledge in a *negative* way in the sense that it can function as a check on false or inappropriate concepts of Jesus.

We believe we have the right to appeal to our limited, but real, historical knowledge of Jesus. The true kerygmatic Christ, the justifiable faith-image, is that consistent with the historical Jesus. The significance of the historical Jesus for Christian faith is that knowledge of this Jesus may be used as a means of testing the claims of the Christs presented in the competing kerygmata to be Jesus Christ. To this limited extent our historical knowledge of Jesus validates the Christian kerygma; it does not validate it as *kerygma,* but it validates it as Christian.[173]

What Perrin means is that the need to distinguish between true and false faith-images of Jesus is always present. *Historical knowledge serves a vital role by providing information that falsifies unhistorical pictures of Jesus.*

Third, Perrin suggests, historical knowledge can be relevant to faith knowledge by helping believers of later generations to enter into a relationship with the person and teaching of Jesus that approximates that of the early church. In other words, it is possible for a believer in any age and culture to hear Jesus' message stated in a form relevant to his situation. Perrin's point seems analogous to Søren Kierkegaard's call for people to become "contemporaneous" with Christ. What Kierkegaard meant was that in the context of the dead and sterile orthodoxy of his Danish Lutheranism, many members of Christendom thought of Jesus and the cross exclusively as historical events and nothing more. What is required, Kierkegaard thought, is for people to leap the centuries and become contemporaneous with Christ.

Alternatives to Perrin's Position

It is interesting to note that Perrin regarded his Bultmannian position as essentially a centrist view that mediates between more extreme views on both the right and the left. To the right of Perrin are thinkers like Joachim Jeremias who think historical knowledge is more directly related to and constitutive of faith knowledge, a position I share. Conservatives take history more seriously than Perrin and Bultmann, seriously enough at least to allow that if the resurrection of Jesus had never occurred, faith in Christ is the useless exercise that Paul describes in 1 Corinthians 15:12–19.

To the left of Perrin are thinkers like Karl Jaspers and Schubert Ogden. While those more conservative than Perrin tie faith knowledge more closely to historical knowledge, those to his left blur the difference between faith knowledge and historic knowledge. For these more radical thinkers, knowledge of Jesus cannot be qualitatively different from knowledge of other persons in history. If, as the radicals maintain, a faith knowledge is only a variant of historic knowledge, Jesus becomes only one of a class of historic figures, a view that effectively destroys his uniqueness within history. Perrin objects. Christ is unique, and therefore the most appropriate form of knowledge of him (faith knowledge) is distinct from the historic knowledge we have of other important events and people.

The Testing of Faith Knowledge

Unlike historical knowledge, which is tested by criteria provided by scientific historiography, "reli-

gious or faith-knowledge . . . should be subject to
quite different tests: the understanding of ultimate
reality it mediates, the kind of religious experience it
inspires, the quality of personal and communal life it
makes possible, and so on.''[174] But Perrin also admits
the relevance of an empirical historical test for faith
knowledge. Faith knowledge, he writes, "may also
be subjected to the tests of determining whether or not
the knowledge is also factual or true in an empirical
sense, so far as any such test is possible in connection
with it, but it must always be recognized that although
historical knowledge can have this kind of significance, this kind of significance is not limited to
knowledge that is also historical.''[175]

There are a number of reasons why thinkers like
Bultmann and Perrin are reluctant to relate faith
knowledge too closely to historical knowledge. To
put it candidly, some of the more important of these
considerations appear to pertain to the naturalistic
philosophic and liberal theological presuppositions
that operate at the foundations of their thought. Seldom, if ever, do they acknowledge these presuppositions; perhaps Butlmann and Perrin were not fully
conscious of them. Both writers express concern
about making something as important as Christian
faith subject to the vicissitudes and possible falsification of historical knowledge. Doing this, Paul Van
Buren warned, would place the Christian "at the
mercy of the historian, so that if historical judgment
were to repaint the picture of Jesus, the character or
content of faith would have to shift with the historical
reconstruction.''[176] After all, the argument goes, history can never provide certainty. The results of historical investigation are always probable, subject to
revision and possible falsification. Is not the vacillat-
ing, shifting, and uncertain foundation of history a
questionable ground for something as important as
one's hope for heaven? Does it make sense to rest
anything so important on something so unstable?
Hence, thinkers like Bultmann believe they have done
Christianity a favor by freeing it from this risk by
making it immune to historical falsification.

The particular kind of immunity sought by

Bultmann and his followers carries a high price tag. It does not secure the intellectual respectability Bultmann sought. If all one cares about is attaining psychological assurance about the Christian faith, it is not necessary to study either history or Bultmann's theory. All one need do is hire a good hypnotist. The same psychological certainty desired by Bultmann can be gained simply by hypnotizing people into a state of "faith."

The conservative should be willing to bite the bullet and live with risk because he sees there is no immunity from the possibility of doubt in life. As William Hordern once observed:

> When God became man, he entered into all the limitations of human life, which means that he also entered the limitations of history. He who would try to "save" the faith from this kind of historical limitation is trying to tear asunder what God himself has joined together. The Christian is by no means asked to leap in the dark, but he is called to make his decisions within the framework of history where there are no absolute answers.[177]

Theologian Michael Cook gives two good reasons for rejecting the attempt to dissociate faith from the specter of historical risk. For one thing, faith itself involves an essential element of risk. And second, faith by its very nature is historical in the sense that it has an intrinsic or essential relationship to history.

> Faith is a risk precisely because it draws us ever more deeply into the human and the historical. In other words, God is to be found not in opposition to but at the very center of our humanness *qua* historical . . . faith itself, *qua* historical, is the risk. Faith does not give us the kind of certainty that would either remove all doubt and risk from the commitment one makes or remove one from involvement in the historical in making the commitment. Yet, it does give us certainty, the kind of certainty that allows us to trust in a promised future.[178]

A similar view is advanced by Protestant Arlie J. Hoover:

> History and faith, therefore, are closely akin because both demand the attitude of trust before you can use them at all. We believe in order to understand. The

layman must trust the work of the historian; the historian must trust his witnesses and his documents; even the witnesses must have first trusted their own senses. This trust, like any kind of faith, isn't credulity or gullibility; there are sufficient reasons to put stock in it, but it still doesn't reach the level of rational [that is, logical] certainty.[179]

According to Hoover, history wears two faces, one objective and the other subjective. This dual nature of history enables it to overcome the excesses of both mysticism and positivism.

> History avoids *mysticism* . . . because it insists that the historical event isn't totally subjective. An event usually occurred back there, and thus it isn't locked up in anyone's mind. Having occurred objectively, it is from then on available to all inquiring minds. Furthermore, your apprehension of an event can be verbalized and described; it isn't ineffable, for you can tell others of the event and invite them to examine it. Those who complain that religion should be universally known to all men overlook the fact that a historical event, by being objective, is potentially a universal truth.[180]

Thus history avoids the subjectivism of mysticism because it has an objective dimension. But history also avoids the excesses of positivism because it has a subjective side. The past cannot be experienced directly; it can be encountered only through the medium of records. Unless the historian believes in his authorities, he cannot take one step.

> History and faith go hand in hand, because together they combine the best elements of rationalism and [subjectivism]. They create a subtle balance between knowledge and hope, a beneficent tension between reason and will, analysis and choice, head and heart, logic and axiologic. . . . Just as faith is a state of conviction midway between certainty and credulity, so history is a mode of revelation midway between (1) total disclosure of God and (2) total concealment of God. Those who seek God with a pure heart and an open mind will find him in history, I believe, for his revelation there is adequate. But for those who have already made up their minds that they won't believe, history is unconvincing; they gleefully point to its uncertainty, its contingency, its lack of demonstration.[181]

On this view, then, faith and history cannot get along without each other. Without historical knowledge, the kind of faith described in the New Testament cannot exist. But without faith, there cannot be historical knowledge. Faith is a necessary precondition for historical knowledge. Faith and history are interdependent.

Historical Knowledge and Interpersonal Knowledge

Neoorthodox theologians like Emil Brunner and existentialist theologians like Bultmann grounded many of their claims on the assumption that I-Thou knowledge (as opposed to the kind of subject-object relationship found in I-It knowledge) is the paradigm of religious knowledge. In other words, they disparaged cognitive knowledge in which a human being relates to objectively true propositions and interpreted divine revelation after the model of interpersonal human dialogue. The dichotomy between I-Thou and I-It knowledge in religion can be faulted on many grounds.* To mention just one, the appeal of this position to the model of interpersonal human dialogue is misleading insofar as it suggests that I-Thou knowledge is totally divorced from I-It knowledge. It is impossible for two human beings to have a meaningful interpersonal relationship without some prior knowledge *about* each other.

This dependence of I-Thou knowledge upon I-It knowledge is just as apparent in history. Two people can never have a really close interpersonal relationship without some knowledge of each other's history. Catholic scholar Michael Cook explains:

> When two people meet one another they go through a kind of historical-critical process in getting to know one another (namely, background, interests, etc.) but if they are to move beyond a merely superficial relationship to something more deeply human there comes a point at which they must be able to make a faith commitment on the basis of what is known about the other person, but the commitment itself transcends the kind of evidence which would prove to oneself or to anyone else that such a

---

*See, for example, Ronald Nash, *The Word of God and the Mind of Man.*

commitment should be made. The moment of trust is a moment of transcendence, a willingness to step "beyond" what can be strictly proved and make a fundamental affirmation of the goodness of the other person. As such, it is a great risk to oneself because it is at that very moment that one is the most vulnerable.[182]

Cook is right. Amid the idle chatter that often characterizes the conversation of two people beginning to feel an attraction for each other can be found inevitable questions about the other person's *history*. It seems, then, that genuine interpersonal knowledge is impossible apart from historical knowledge. To whatever extent faith knowledge is analogous to interpersonal human knowledge, it is obvious that a faith commitment requires prior historical knowledge. Trust is inseparable from knowledge. When a person becomes a friend or falls in love, he makes a commitment that goes beyond what he knows; but nonetheless the commitment would never have been made without some prior knowledge. The person making the commitment reasons that even though there may be much about this person he does not know, he knows enough to believe, to trust, to make a commitment that goes beyond the evidence. But the commitment is still based on some evidence.

Given the tendency of so many contemporary theologians to exclude cognitive knowledge from religious experience, Cook's point is important. Historical knowledge, it turns out, is an important precondition of interpersonal knowledge. But historical knowledge continues to be relevant even after a commitment is made. Suppose one person who makes a commitment to another discovers that what was believed about the history of the other is false. For example, imagine a person whose father died shortly before his birth. Over the years, as this person grew into young manhood, he was told many stories about his deceased father that represented him as courageous, noble, and virtuous. Holding a faith-image of his father as a great man, the young man is understandably proud of his father; he believes *in* his father. But now suppose that the young man discovers that all of the stories about his father are false; his father in truth was just the opposite of what the young man believed him to be. Dare we hold in this case, as theologians like Bultmann appear to suggest in the case of Jesus, that the historical truth is irrelevant to the son's faith in his father? In the case of any normal and reasonable person, we would expect that the correction of the man's false historical knowledge about his father would destroy his faith knowledge in his father. Why should the relationship of faith knowledge to historical knowledge be any different in belief in Jesus Christ? Changes in our historical knowledge can change and even destroy interpersonal relationships. This is the way it is in nonreligious dimensions of life; and this is the way it is in religion.

Models of Faith

Our discussion of the relationship of faith to historical knowledge can be concluded with a consideration of several models of faith. Several such analogies can illuminate even further the interdependence of faith and history.

1. Faith can be compared to the physical act of leaning or resting. Faith is a kind of surrender or commitment illustrated by the act of resting one's entire weight on some support. When a person prepares to sit, he is about to commit his entire weight to a chair. When a person sits, he exercises the faith that the chair is strong enough to support his weight. A person who believed that a chair could not support his weight but then proceeded to sit anyway is not exactly the model of a rational human being. This model of faith strongly suggests faith's need for objective support, the kind of support provided by history.

2. Faith may also be compared to walking on a tightrope. In other words, it is a balancing act. As Arlie Hoover suggests, faith "strikes a delicate balance between rationalism and fideism, reason and trust, evidence and commitment, head and heart . . . fact and value."[183] The key to success in such an enterprise is maintaining one's balance. Tightrope walkers often lean dangerously to one side because they sense they are in danger of falling; a drastic tilt in the other direction is necessary to prevent the fall.

Depending on changing conditions in our culture, a tilt to one side or the other may be necessary in order to assure our balance. Kierkegaard's culture was leaning dangerously toward an impersonal rationalism. Anyone who has read Kierkegaard knows how extreme his tilt to the subjecive side was. In fact, it was so extreme that he is often misrepresented as an irrationalist and a subjectivist. In our day, the tilt has been toward a subjectivism and irrationalism so severe that a compensating tilt toward rationalism seems justified.*

3. Faith may also be thought of in terms of a leap. First of all, faith can be compared to leaping because it requires that the believer go beyond available evidence. If we never trusted beyond the evidence available to us, we would never get very far in life. Most of our beliefs require us to go beyond the evidence to some extent. David Hume's analysis of scientific law is a good example of this. Hume asked how we know that the future will be like the past. Even though we might know that the sun has heretofore always risen in the east, can we really *know* that the sun will rise in the east tomorrow? Hume's question raises a fundamental point about scientific knowledge. Given our assumptions about the laws of nature, we develop a confidence that nature will continue to behave in an orderly, regular way; we come to assume that the future will be like the past. But what is the ground for this confidence? Every law of science says more than the evidence warrants; the evidence can tell us only what has happened up to the present, whereas laws of science predict what will continue to happen in the future. Since we can have evidence only for what has already happened, it follows that no available evidence can possibly ground scientific predictions about the future. According to Hume, what really grounds

---

*Once again I am constrained to mention that I have discussed the drift of modern theology in irrationalism and subjectivism in my book *The Word of God and the Mind of Man*. My book also outlines what is necessary to restore a proper balance, namely a recovery of confidence that the human mind is capable of attaining cognitive knowledge about the mind of God and that God has revealed true propositions in His Word.

"scientific" claims about the future is faith.* Our confidence that the sun will rise in the east tomorrow isn't really based on evidence; an act of faith is required to take us from the evidence of what has happened in the past to what we believe or trust will happen in the future. Religious faith obviously includes a similar kind of leap. Paul said that for the present, we see only a poor reflection (1 Cor. 13:12). According to the writer of Hebrews, "Faith is being sure of what we hope for and certain of what we do not see" (Heb. 11:1 NIV). Faith, then, can be compared to a leap in the sense that it involves a commitment that goes beyond available evidence.

Much of the confusion about regarding faith as a leap results from imagining faith as a kind of single gigantic leap into a dark, apparently bottomless chasm. Anyone who leaps off a cliff not knowing how far it is to the bottom is not a paradigm of the man or woman of faith. He is either crazy or stupid. When Søren Kierkegaard talked about faith as a leap, the image he had in mind was that of *skipping*. When a person skips, he is on the ground, then off the ground, and then back on the ground again. He can never be off the ground for very long. It is in this sense that faith can be compared to leaping. We must never get very far from our evidence, from our objective ground of support. We have to keep coming back to something solid. History provides the kind of solid support required by the man or woman of faith.

Finally, faith can be compared to a leap in another sense because like leaping, faith requires a solid jumping-off point. People who doubt this should try leaping off a water bed. If faith is a leap, then there must be something solid to support that leap. There must always be grounds or reasons or evidence to support the faith initially.

Conclusion

This chapter has examined the questions, What is the relationship between individual Christian faith and history? Is Christian faith totally dependent on history

---

*Hume explained faith in a rather peculiar way, using synonyms like habit and custom. But that is another matter.

or totally independent? We have seen that faith of any kind and history are *interdependent* in more ways than many people realize. Personal faith or trust in other people often proceeds on the basis of beliefs *about* that person's history. When that historical knowledge is shown to be false, *belief in* that person can be weakened or destroyed. The kind of personal faith and trust that grounds human friendship and love has an inherent historical component. The person who trusts and loves another naturally wants to know more about the other person's history. Historical knowledge of this kind can cause trust and love to grow or can lead it to die. Christians are people who have a loving trust in God and in His Son, Jesus Christ. Their faith and trust also have an inherent historical component. From its inception, Christianity has been a religion with a past. Without that past, Christians could have no grounded hope for the future.

Response

Response

The old axiom "seeing is believing" is still with us. Some areas of science have the advantage of repeating an experiment if it is not believed by the observer. On the other hand the discipline of history does not have such luxury. A given historical event cannot be repeated, but if it was witnessed and reported by reliable witnesses, one must believe it happened. But herein is the problem: the historian is not able to know his subject directly and must interpret what is recorded by those witnesses. In the effort to recover what has been reported, Dr. Nash carefully examines the attempts by the various historians and theologians in this most difficult task. It is true that every historian has his biases, but he should not let them determine what is acceptable and unacceptable. Nash has shown that there has been on the part of many modern historians a bias against the possibility of the supernatural, so that they predetermine that anything beyond the naturalistic world must be seen as inauthentic.

Furthermore, there is a skepticism toward the recorded events and sayings in the New Testament on the part of some theologians. Nash has demonstrated that this has been true among many of the form critics like Bultmann, who felt that many of the sayings of Jesus were created by the early church. Thus the form critics must ask whether a saying of Jesus was actually spoken by Jesus during his ministry or was an invention by the early church that is attributed to Jesus. However, this skepticism is carried even further by the redaction critic who posits that each of the Gospel writers is an author or redactor in his own right rather than a mere collector of materials of the early community as posited by form critics. This means that the author of a Gospel may have invented sayings of Jesus, for it is felt by some redaction critics that the Lord who spoke in his ministry is the Lord who was speaking by means of the Gospel author.[184]

So the redaction critic asks whether a particular

HAROLD W. HOEHNER

157

saying attributed to Jesus was actually spoken by Jesus in his ministry, whether it was an invention by the early church, or whether it was an invention of the particular author of the Gospel. Hence, some of the redaction critics are quite pessimistic in that all we know about Jesus from the Gospels is but a faint "whisper of his voice" and we can "trace in them but the outskirts of his ways."[185] Even more starkly Perrin states, "It raises above all the question as to whether the view of the historical Jesus as the locus of revelation and the central concern of Christian faith is in fact justifiable, and it raises this question because it shows how truly foreign such a view is to the New Testament itself."[186] But form and redaction critics have overstepped their bounds, for they judge the content by its form or by criteria set up by the modern theologian. They will not let the text speak on its own terms. Certainly the modern theologians would not want us to read their books the way they want us to read the New Testament!

All of this is dealing with the historian trying to recover the historical Jesus from the written materials. Nash has done a great service in helping us in this with skill and accuracy. On the other hand he says very little with respect to the credibility of the eyewitnesses and/or the authors of the Gospels. He may not have wanted to do this, first, because it is a vast subject in itself and could well have been beyond the scope of this monograph and, second, because it has already been discussed in another book in this series.[187] However, as Sherwin-White has pointed out, the New Testament critics tend to be far more pessimistic than the classical historians regarding the reliability of their sources.[188] If the classical historians would treat the historical sources the way many New Testament scholars do, we would know much less—possibly nothing—about Alexander the Great, Julius Caesar, Augustus, Tiberius, etc., because the accounts are often so diverse and contradictory and are often recorded by those of other generations than those in which these historic figures lived.

Dr. Nash's competence as a historian is clearly seen in his dealing with the problems of historiography. He is very careful not to give simplistic solutions to complex problems. He has helped us to evaluate our methods of deciphering what has been written. His lucid treatment aids us to say no more and no less than what the documents record.

References

References

[1] William Hordern, *New Directions in Theology Today, I, Introduction* (Philadelphia: Westminster, 1966), p. 55

[2] Herbert Butterfield, *Christianity and History* (London, Bell, 1949), p. 3.

[3] Ibid., p. 119.

[4] T. A. Roberts, *History and Christian Apologetic* (London: SPCK, 1960), p. vii.

[5] Alan Richardson, *Christian Apologetics* (London: SCM, 1947), p. 91.

[6] W. H. Walsh, *Philosophy of History: An Introduction* (New York: Harper & Row, 1960), p. 31.

[7] Carl E. Braaten, *History and Hermeneutics* (Philadelphia: Westminster, 1966), pp. 38–39.

[8] James Peter, *Finding the Historical Jesus* (New York: Harper & Row, 1965), p. 174.

[9] John Macquarrie, *An Existentialist Theology* (New York: Harper Torchbooks, 1965), pp. 166, 171.

[10] Braaten, *History and Hermeneutics*, p. 39.

[11] See the preface to the first edition of Ranke's *Histories of the Latin and Germanic Nations from 1494 to 1514* (1909; reprint ed., New York: AMS, n.d.).

[12] Braaten, *History and Hermeneutics*, p. 55.

[13] I. Howard Marshall, *I Believe in the Historical Jesus* (Grand Rapids: Eerdmans, 1977), pp. 110–11.

[14] George Tyrrell, *Christianity at the Cross-Roads* (New York: Longmans, Green, 1910), p. 44.

[15] Braaten, *History and Hermeneutics*, p. 55.

[16] T. A. Roberts, *History and Christian Apologetics*, p. x.

[17] Alan Richardson, *History, Sacred and Profane* (Philadelphia: Westminster, 1964), pp. 184–85.

[18] Van Austen Harvey, *The Historian and the Believer* (New York: Macmillan, 1969), p. 168.

[19] Braaten, *History and Hermeneutics*, pp. 66–67.

[20] Ibid., p. 38.

[21] Cited in Ronald Nash, ed., *Ideas of History*, vol. 2. (New York: Dutton, 1969), p. 31.

[22] Croce's views can be found in chapter 1 of his *History: Its Theory and Practice,* trans. D. Ainslie (reprint; New York: Russell and Russell, 1960).

[23] R. G. Collingwood, *The Idea of History* (New York: Oxford University Press, 1956), p. 213.

[24] Ibid., p. 218.

[25] Ibid., p. 215.

[26] Ibid.

[27] Walsh, *Philosophy of History,* p. 59.

[28] Ibid., p. 57.

[29] Ibid., p. 58.

[30] Norman Sykes, "Some Current Conceptions of Historiography and their Significance for Christian Apologetic," *Journal of Theological Studies* 50 (1949), 32.

[31] Ibid., p. 33.

[32] William Manson, *Jesus the Messiah* (London: Hodder & Stoughton, 1943), p. 162.

[33] T. A. Roberts, *History and Christian Apologetic,* p. 9.

[34] Ibid., p. 20.

[35] In *Theories of History,* ed. P. Gardiner (New York: Free Press, 1959).

[36] W. H. Walsh, "Meaning in History," in *Theories of History,* p. 298.

[37] William Dray, "The Historical Explanation of Actions Reconsidered," *Philosophy and History,* ed. Sidney Hook (New York: New York University Press, 1963); reprinted in Nash, *Ideas of History,* 2:109.

[38] Rudolf Bultmann, *History and Eschatology: The Presence of Eternity* (New York: Harper and Brothers, 1957), p. 155.

[39] Rudolf Bultmann, *Jesus and the Word* (New York: Scribner, 1934), p. 8.

[40] Rudolf Bultmann, *Jesus Christ and Mythology* (New York: Scribner, 1958), p. 15.

[41] Ibid.

[42] Ibid., p. 21.

[43] Ibid.

[44] Ibid., p. 15.

[45] Ibid., p. 37.

[46] Ibid.

[47]Karl Jaspers, "Myth and Christianity" in *Myth and Christianity* by Karl Jaspers and Rudolf Bultmann (New York: Noonday, 1958), p. 5.

[48]Ibid., pp. 5–6.

[49]See Bultmann, *Jesus Christ and Mythology,* p. 19.

[50]Ibid., p. 15.

[51]Ibid.

[52]Ibid., p. 19.

[53]Rudolf Bultmann, *Existence and Faith,* ed. Schubert M. Ogden (New York: Meridian, 1960), pp. 291–92.

[54]Thomas F. Torrance, *Space, Time and Resurrection* (Grand Rapids: Eerdmans, 1976), p. 4.

[55]John Macquarrie, "Rudolf Bultmann," *A Handbook of Christian Theologians* (Cleveland: World, 1967), p. 448.

[56]Bultmann, *Jesus Christ and Mythology,* p. 36.

[57]Ibid., p. 45.

[58]Bultmann, *History and Eschatology,* p. 155.

[59]Norman Perrin, *Rediscovering the Teaching of Jesus* (New York: Harper & Row, 1967), p. 221.

[60]Rudolf Bultmann, *Kerygma and Myth,* ed. H. W. Bartsch, trans. R. H. Fuller (London: SPCK, 1953), 1:210–11.

[61]Basil Mitchell, *The Justification of Religious Belief* (New York: Seabury, 1973), pp. 141–42.

[62]I. Howard Marshall, *I Believe in the Historical Jesus* (Grand Rapids: Eerdmans, 1977), pp. 72–73.

[63]Braaten, *History and Hermeneutics,* pp. 132–33.

[64]Bultmann, *History and Eschatology,* p. 184.

[65]Bultmann, *Jesus and the Word,* p. 3.

[66]Kenneth Kantzer, "The Christ-Revelation as Act and Interpretation," in *Jesus of Nazareth: Saviour and Lord,* ed. Carl F. H. Henry (Grand Rapids: Eerdmans, 1966), p. 258.

[67]Bultmann, *Jesus and the Word,* p. 11.

[68]Perrin, *Rediscovering the Teaching of Jesus,* p. 16.

[69]R. H. Lightfoot, *History and Interpretation in the Gospels* (New York: Harper and Brothers, n.d.), p. 225.

[70]A. N. Sherwin-White, *Roman Society and Roman Law in the New Testament* (New York: Oxford University Press, 1963), p. 187.

[71] See Norman Perrin, *What Is Redaction Criticism?* (Philadelphia: Fortress, 1969), p. 69.

[72] Charles C. Anderson, *Critical Quests of Jesus* (Grand Rapids: Eerdmans, 1969), p. 104.

[73] D. M. Baillie, *God Was in Christ* (New York: Scribner, 1948), p. 57.

[74] Perrin, *What Is Redaction Criticism?* p. 16.

[75] Perrin, *Rediscovering the Teaching of Jesus,* p. 21.

[76] Perrin, *What Is Redaction Criticism?* p. 29.

[77] Birger Gerhardsson, *Memory and Manuscript* (Gleerup: Lund, 1961), p. 209.

[78] R. T. France, "The Authenticity of the Sayings of Jesus," in *History, Criticism and Faith,* ed. Colin Brown (Downers Grove, Ill.: InterVarsity, 1976), pp. 125–26.

[79] William G. Doty, "The Discipline and Literature of New Testament Form Criticism," *Anglican Theological Review* 51 (1969), 304. Doty's important article is on pages 257–319.

[80] Ibid.

[81] See Perrin, *Rediscovering the Teaching of Jesus,* p. 39.

[82] Joachim Jeremias, *New Testament Theology* (London: SCM, 1971), p. 37.

[83] Neil J. McEleney, "Authenticating Criteria and Mark 7,1–23," *Catholic Biblical Quarterly* 34 (1972), 446–47.

[84] Jeremias, *New Testament Theology,* p. 37.

[85] Robert H. Stein, "What is *Redaktionsgeschichte?*" *Journal of Biblical Literaure* 88 (1969): 46. Stein's article (contained on pages 45–56 of this journal) provides an excellent introduction to the subject. Another standard source, written by an advocate of redaction criticism who is also skeptical of the historical reliability of the Gospels is Perrin, *What Is Redaction Criticism?*

[86] Perrin, *What Is Redaction Criticism?* p. 1.

[87] Stephen S. Smalley, "Redaction Criticism" in *New Testament Interpretation,* ed. I. Howard Marshall (Grand Rapids: Eerdmans, 1977), pp. 181–95.

[88] Ibid., p. 181.

[89] Ibid., p. 188.

[90] Ibid., pp. 188–89.

[91]Ibid., p. 189.

[92]William L. Lane, *"Redaktionsgeschichte* and the De-Historicizing of the New Testament Gospel," *Bulletin of the Evangelical Theological Society* 11 (1968): 32.

[93]A number of evangelical assessments of redaction criticism are available. They include: Smalley, "Redaction Criticism"; Lane, *"Redaktionsgeschichte* and the De-Historicizing of the New Testament Gospel"; Roger Mohrlang, "Redaction Criticism and the Gospel of Mark: An Evaluation of the Work of Willi Marxsen, *Studia Biblica et Theologica* 6 (1976): 18–33; Robert H. Gundry, "A Theological Postscript," in Gundry, *Matthew: A Commentary on His Literary and Theological Art* (Grand Rapids: Eerdmans, 1982), pp. 623–40; Ralph P. Martin, *New Testament Foundations,* 2 vols. (Grand Rapids, Eerdmans, 1975), 1:136–38; D. A. Carson, "Redaction Criticism: On the Legitimacy and Illegitimacy of a Literary Tool," in *Scripture and Truth,* ed. D. A. Carson and John D. Woodbridge (Grand Rapids: Zondervan, 1983), pp. 119–42; Grant R. Osborne, "The Evangelical and Redaction Criticism: Critique and Methodology," *Journal of the Evangelical Theological Society* 22 (1979): 305–22; Robert E. Morosco, "Redaction Criticism and the Evangelical: Matthew 10 a Test Case," *Journal of the Evangelical Theological Society* 22 (1979): 323–31; Grant R. Osborne, "The Evangelical and *Traditions-geschichte*," *Journal of the Evangelical Theological Society* 21 (1978): 117–30; Grant R. Osborne, "Redaction Criticism and the Great Commission: A Case Study Toward a Biblial Understanding of Inerrancy," *Journal of the Evangelical Theological Society* 19 (1976): 73–85; Marshall, *I Believe in the Historical Jesus,* pp. 156–61.

[94]Max Fisch, "The Philosophy of History: A Dialogue," *Philosophy* (Tokyo: 1959), p. 167.

[95]Beard, in Nash, *The Word of God,* p. 173.

[96]Ibid., p 171.

[97]Harvey, *The Historian and the Believer,* pp. 211–12.

[98]Ibid., p. 213.

[99]See Morton White, *Social Thought in America* (New York: Viking, 1949), pp. 220–35.

[100]Norman Geisler, *Christian Apologetics* (Grand Rapids, Baker, 1976), p. 297.

[101]Ibid.

[102]Nills Alstrup Dahl, "The Problem of the Historical

Jesus," in *Kerygma and History,* ed. Carl E. Braaten and Roy A. Harrisville (New York: Abingdon, 1961), p. 150.

[103]George Eldon Ladd, *I Believe in the Resurrection of Jesus* (Grand Rapids: Eerdmans, 1975), pp. 12–13.

[104]Ibid., p. 13.

[105]Ibid.

[106]Ibid.

[107]Carl Becker's article, "What Are Historical Facts?" was originally published in *The Western Political Quarterly* 8 (1955). It has been reprinted in Ronald H. Nash, *Ideas of History* 2 vols. (New York: Dutton, 1969), 2:177–93.

[108]T. A. Roberts, *History and Christian Apologetic,* p. x.

[109]Becker, "What Are Historical Facts?" p. 179.

[110]Ibid.

[111]Ibid., p. 181.

[112]Ibid., p. 182.

[113]Ibid.

[114]Richardson, *Christian Apologetics,* p. 145.

[115]Maurice Mandelbaum, *The Problem of Historical Knowledge* (New York: Harper & Row, 1967), p. 97.

[116]James Robinson, "The Revelation of God in Jesus," in *Theology as History,* ed. James Robinson and John B. Cobb, Jr. (New York: Harper & Row, 1967), pp. 126–27. It would be a mistake to assume that any agreement with Robinson on this point implies sympathy with his theological position in general.

[117]Ibid., p. 127.

[118]William Hamilton, "The Character of Pannenberg's Theology," in *Theology as History,* p. 181.

[119]Richardson, *Christian Apologetics,* p. 146.

[120]Kantzer, "The Christ-Revelation," p. 257.

[121]Oscar Cullmann, "The Resurrection: Event and Meaning," *Christianity Today* 9 (1965): 8.

[122]Oscar Cullmann, *Salvation in History* (London: SCM, 1967), p. 90.

[123]Richardson, *Christian Apologetics,* pp. 146–47.

[124]Richardson, *History,* p. 198.

[125]A. M. Ramsey, *The Resurrection of Christ* (London: Bles, 1945), pp. 7–8.

[126]Ladd, *Resurrection of Jesus.*

127Daniel Fuller, *Easter Faith and History* (Grand Rapids: Eerdmans, 1965), p. 145.

128Ladd, *Resurrection of Jesus,* pp. 18ff.

129Braaten, *History and Hermeneutics,* pp. 82–83.

130Bultmann, *Kerygma and Myth,* 1:39.

131Ibid., p. 42.

132Kantzer, "The Christ-Revelation," p. 249.

133Braaten, *History and Hermeneutics,* p. 92.

134Ibid., pp. 86–87.

135Schubert Ogden, *Christ Without Myth* (New York: Harper and Brothers, 1961), p. 136.

136Braaten, *History and Hermeneutics,* p. 85.

137Ibid., pp. 83–84.

138See the discussion in Peter Selby, *Look for the Living* (Philadelphia: Fortress, 1976), pp. 46–47.

139See, for example, Barth's *Church Dogmatics* III, 2, pp. 437ff.

140Ibid., III, 2, p. 448.

141Ibid., I, 2, pp. 114ff. and I, i, p. 373.

142Ibid., III, 2, p. 446.

143Ibid., I, 2, pp. 114ff.

144Kantzer, "The Christ-Revelation," p. 249.

145Ibid., p. 251.

146Daniel Fuller, *Easter Faith and History,* pp. 149–50.

147Ibid., p. 161.

148Ibid., pp. 165–66.

149Wolfhart Pannenberg, *Faith and Reality,* tr. John Maxwell (Philadelphia: Westminster, 1977), p. 72.

150Ibid.

151Wolfhart Pannenberg, *Revelation as History* (New York: Macmillan, 1968), p. 135.

152Daniel Fuller, *Easter Faith and History,* p. 184.

153Ibid., p. 187.

154Ibid.

155Ladd, *Resurrection of Jesus,* p. 96.

156Ibid., p. 94.

157Ibid., p. 96.

158Ibid., p. 98.

[159]Ibid., p. 101.

[160]Ibid., p. 21.

[161]Ibid., p. 12.

[162]Ibid., p. 10.

[163]Ibid., p. 27.

[164]Ibid., pp. 24–25.

[165]Richardson, *History*, p. 200.

[166]Perin, *Rediscovering the Teaching of Jesus*, pp. 234ff.

[167]Ibid., p. 235.

[168]Ibid.

[169]Ibid., p. 237.

[170]Ibid., pp. 237–38.

[171]Marshall, *I Believe in the Historical Jesus*, pp. 44–45.

[172]Perrin, *Rediscovering the Teaching of Jesus*, p. 244.

[173]Ibid.

[174]Ibid., p. 241.

[175]Ibid.

[176]Paul Van Buren, *The Secular Meaning of the Gospel* (New York: Macmillan, 1963), pp. 124–25.

[177]Hordern, *New Directions in Theology Today*, p. 55.

[178]Michael L. Cook, S.J., *The Jesus of Faith* (New York: Paulist, 1981), p. 25.

[179]Arlie J. Hoover, *Dear Agnos: A Defense of Christianity* (Grand Rapids: Baker, 1976), p. 122.

[180]Ibid.

[181]Ibid., p. 123

[182]Cook, *The Jesus of Faith*, pp. 25–26.

[183]Hoover, *Dear Agnos*, p. 37

[184]Perrin, *Redaction Criticism*, p. 73–78

[185]Lightfoot, *History and Interpretation*, p. 225.

[186]Perrin, *Redaction Criticism*, p. 72.

[187]Jon A. Buell and O. Quentin Hyder, *Jesus: God, Ghost or Guru?* (Grand Rapids: Zondervan, 1978), p. 41–80.

[188]Sherwin-White, *Roman Society and Roman Law*, pp. 172–93.

For Further Reading

For Further Reading

Brown, Colin, ed. **History, Criticism and Faith.** Downers Grove, Ill.: InterVarsity, 1976.

Four evangelical scholars including F. F. Bruce cover a number of important issues regarding Christianity's relationship with history.

Henry, Carl F. H. **God, Revelation and Authority.** 6 vols. Waco: Word, 1976, vol. 2.

One of a projected six-volume series, the last six chapters of this volume focus on the subject of God's revelation in history.

Henry, Carl F. H., ed. **Jesus of Nazareth: Saviour and Lord.** Grand Rapids, Eerdmans, 1967.

An anthology of essays by a team of outstanding evangelical scholars that covers most of the questions students ask about the historical Jesus.

Ladd, George Eldon. **I Believe in the Resurrection of Jesus.** Grand Rapids: Eerdmans, 1975.

An oft-published New Testament scholar gives his reasons for believing in the historicity of the Resurrection.

Marsden, George, and Roberts, Frank, eds. **A Christian View of History?** Grand Rapids, Eerdmans, 1975.

A group of Christian historians, philosophers, and theologians consider problems involved in developing a Christian view of history. The book contains a helpful bibliographic essay.

Marshall, I. Howard **I Believe in the Historical Jesus.** Grand Rapids: Eerdmans, 1977.

A respected British scholar considers why it is reasonable to believe in the historical Jesus.

Nash, Ronald H. **Ideas of History.** 2 vols. New York: Dutton, 1969.

An anthology of readings in both the speculative and critical philosophy of history. This book contains much of the philosophical material cited in my book.

Roberts, Robert C. **Rudolf Bultmann's Theology.** Grand Rapids: Eerdmans, 1976.

Robert's book is one of the most important critiques of Bultmann's thought.